FILM FOCUS

Ronald Gottesman and Harry M. Geduld
General Editors

THE FILM FOCUS SERIES PRESENTS THE BEST THAT HAS BEEN WRITTEN ABOUT THE ART OF FILM AND THE MEN WHO CREATED IT. COMBINING CRITICISM WITH HISTORY, BIOGRAPHY, AND ANALYSIS OF TECHNIQUE, THE VOLUMES IN THE SERIES EXPLORE THE MANY DIMENSIONS OF THE FILM MEDIUM AND ITS IMPACT ON MODERN SOCIETY.

WILLIAM JOHNSON, *editor of this volume in the Film Focus series, is a British-born magazine editor who has spent many years studying the film scene in London, Paris, and New York. He has written extensively on film for various publications and has also published articles on science fiction.*

FOCUS ON

THE
SCIENCE FICTION
FILM

edited by

WILLIAM JOHNSON

A SPECTRUM BOOK

Prentice-Hall, Inc.
Englewood Cliffs, N.J.

Library of Congress Cataloging in Publication Data

JOHNSON, WILLIAM.   comp.
    Focus on the science fiction film.

    (Film focus) (A Spectrum book)
    Bibliography: p.
    1. Moving-pictures—Plots, themes, etc.—Science
fiction. I. Title.
PN1995.9.S26J6   791.43'0909'31   72–3633
ISBN 0–13–795179–5
ISBN 0–13–795161–2 (pbk.)

10   9   8   7   6   5   4   3   2   1

PRENTICE-HALL INTERNATIONAL, INC. (*London*)
PRENTICE-HALL OF AUSTRALIA, PTY. LTD. (*Sydney*)
PRENTICE-HALL OF CANADA, LTD. (*Toronto*)
PRENTICE-HALL OF INDIA PRIVATE LIMITED (*New Delhi*)
PRENTICE-HALL OF JAPAN, INC. (*Tokyo*)

for
Florence
and
Martin

CONTENTS

TAKING STOCK: SOME ISSUES AND ANSWERS

MOVING ON: THE 1960s AND AFTER

ACKNOWLEDGMENTS

More people than I can name have helped with the preparation of this book. I am particularly grateful to Eileen Bowser and the staff of the Film Department of the Museum of Modern Art and to the staff of the Theater Research Department of the New York Public Library at Lincoln Center. Valuable suggestions came from Margaret Ronan, who also provided a number of stills. Philip Thody unraveled some knotty problems of translation. From start to finish, Ronald Gottesman and Harry M. Geduld were generous with encouragement and useful suggestions. Claudia Wilson steered the book through production with tact and skill. My special thanks go to all the authors who consented to have their work appear on these pages, and to the authors and filmmakers who replied to my questionnaires. Finally, my task was made much easier by the encouragement of my wife, and by her patience when I was absorbed in other worlds.

Journey into Science Fiction
by WILLIAM JOHNSON

*"there's a hell of a good universe
next door; let's go"*
—E. E. CUMMINGS

Although science fiction writing has gained enormously in popularity and critical attention in recent years, it is still not fully respectable. Many critics are aware that its subject matter goes far beyond space opera and bug-eyed monsters, but they still complain that its imaginative stamina and literary grace fall short of its initial ideas. Screen science fiction is in an even more dubious position. Its overt subject matter is usually less sophisticated than that of science fiction writing, and is often downright naive or preposterous. Its harshest critics include such champions of science fiction writing as Damon Knight.* When a science fiction film does win extensive praise, it is likely to be viewed (even by its makers) as a special case, not as true science fiction at all: Losey's *The Damned* is an example.

Part of the problem is that it is notoriously hard to frame an adequate, widely acceptable definition of SF (we will use the abbreviation from now on). When applied to films, the term may be used so loosely that it becomes meaningless. It is confusing enough that SF embraces both *Destination Moon,* which glorifies technology, and *Fahrenheit 451,* which relegates it to the background. But a "SF program" offered by a theater or TV station may also include a fantasy adventure like *King Kong,* a supernatural thriller like *Dracula's Daughter,* and a juvenile exercise in special effects like *Attack of the 50 Foot Woman.* There is no clearly recognized border between SF and such genres as fantasy and horror.

Yet this apparent weakness of screen SF may be a sign of strength.

---

* References with a single asterisk will be found in the bibliography. A double asterisk denotes a selection in this book.

1

Gene Youngblood, in *Expanded Cinema,** declares that the Holly-wood genres are dead because their content is, by definition, predict-able. Now, while certain types of SF films (such as those about mon-sters) do indeed fall into familiar patterns, many others do not. In the critical studies contained in this book, the assumptions made about the nature of SF films are varied to the point of contradiction —a good deal more varied than one would expect of assumptions about the nature of the Western or the musical. If Youngblood's thesis is correct, SF films are still vital because no one knows for sure what to expect from them: the genre can still spring surprises.

There is another and more important way in which the territorial vagueness of the SF cinema counts in its favor. While it is often thought of as a dependency of literary SF, the two have developed along quite distinct lines. Historians of literary SF usually trace it back by way of Swift and Kepler as far as Lucian of Samosata, two thousand years ago. It is clear, however, that in historical examples earlier than the nineteenth century, the SF element is invariably a technical device used for didactic and satirical purposes, and that SF plays at best a marginal role in the development of literature. In films the situation is quite different: to a large extent, SF and the cinema developed together. In order to define SF in the cinema, and to understand its relationship to SF writing, we should first look at its history. The selections in this book focus on developments and individual films from the 1890s to the present day, and whether de-scriptive or critical they are, with minor exceptions, arranged in chronological order.

The rapid pace of scientific and technological advances in the nineteenth century led many scientists to believe that the universe was a machine whose workings could, with the right tools, be fully explained. The cinema seemed a typical product of this age of sci-entific confidence. Various lines of discovery—in optics, mechanics, chemistry, and physiology—had converged in its development. More-over, it had been developed partly as a new scientific tool: both Ead-weard Muybridge and Étienne Marey, for example, had devised ways of taking rapid series of photographs in order to analyze animal locomotion.

But right from the beginning the cinema began to evolve into something more independent. Amid the documentary realism of the Lumière brothers' films, there is already a touch of fantasy: in *Charcuterie mécanique* (1895), a comic machine converts live pigs into sausages. Even more significant, the British film pioneer Robert Paul was inspired by H. G. Wells's novel *The Time Machine* (1895) to conceive of presenting a film show as an illusory voyage through time; and Terry Ramsaye suggests that in creating *The Time Machine,* Wells may first have been inspired by the cinema.**

Clearly the film was breaking away from the orderly world of the theater, in which events are seen as they happen. In much the same way and at much the same time, startling new discoveries—X–rays, radioactivity, quantum physics—were bursting out of the orderly world of nineteenth-century science. As Lewis Mumford wrote in *Technics and Civilization* (1934): "The moving picture, with its close-ups and its synoptic views, with its shifting events and its ever-present camera-eye, with its spatial forms always shown through time, with its capacity for representing objects that interpenetrate, and for placing distant environments in immediate juxtaposition . . . with its ability, finally, to represent subjective elements, distortions, hallucinations, is today the only art that can represent with any degree of concreteness the emergent world view that differentiates our culture from every preceding one."

Such philosophical implications of the cinema were, of course, to be discovered only in retrospect. When the Lumières filmed their sausage machine and Paul conceived his Time Machine, they were looking for entertaining ways to catch the public eye. Before long, fiction was dominating the new scientific tool. For many filmmakers and entrepreneurs alike, the cinema was simply an extension of the theater, the music hall, the circus, and the fairground side show. Fiction in the new medium meant popular fiction, emerging as spectacle, sentiment, comedy, and fantasy.

Of these popular ingredients, fantasy played a pivotal role. As the early filmmakers explored the possibilities of the new medium, they discovered various ways in which it could distort reality or present an apparent reality which existed only on film. Georges Méliès is the best known and most prolific of these pioneers, and his first outstanding film was *A Trip to the Moon,* made in 1902.

Seen today, *A Trip to the Moon* is likely to give a first impression of staginess and naiveté. Méliès had no thought of realism; he was intent on devising and playing with various tricks and ideas which would eventually lead not only to science fiction but also to other genres (fantasy, musical, screwball comedy, etc.). Maurice Bessy points out, however,** that Méliès's achievement lay in combining his tricks and flourishes with sustained filmic narratives. That is why

A Trip to the Moon survives. The scenes on the moon, with their giant mushrooms and self-destructing selenites, even today suggest an alien world as much as they do a display of magician's tricks; and the structure of the film—preparation, launching, flight, and landing—creates a sense of space and movement that lifts the viewer out of the stagelike box of Méliès's studio. While Paul failed to develop the cinema into a Time Machine, Méliès successfully revealed its possibilities as a Space Machine.

The time element was there, too. Méliès had learned how to divorce screen time from real time by stopping the camera, rearranging the scene, and restarting the camera as if there had been no break: the film would then contain a magical appearance, disappearance, or metamorphosis. Stuart Blackton in the United States and Emile Cohl in France independently carried this break with real time still further, developing the stop-motion technique for making inanimate objects appear to move. Here again, the new idea paved the way for Mickey Mouse and the puppets of Jiri Trnka as well as for the spacecraft of *2001*. D. W. Griffith came even closer to Paul's dream. His *Man's Genesis* (1911) takes the audience back tens of thousands of years into prehistory, while *Intolerance* (1916) swings them to and fro among four different historical eras. Later, René Clair arrested the flow of time in *Paris Qui Dort (The Crazy Ray,* 1923), showing people frozen in mid-action when put to sleep by an eccentric inventor.

All these films enabled audiences to undergo experiences which were impossible in their normal space-time continuum yet had a startling sense of reality. Many other films offered the impossibility without the realism: in *A Trip to Jupiter* (1909) a king dreams of climbing to the planet Jupiter on a ladder; in *A Trip to Mars* (1910) a scientist is wafted to Mars by a powder that reverses gravity, and is later blown back to Earth by an explosion. A few films turned in the opposite direction, offering new experiences which were or might soon be possible. Thus the British *Battle in the Clouds* (1909) anticipates the Zeppelin bombing raids and aerial dogfights of World War I and the guided missile of more recent times. Feuillade's serials include realistic but still unfamiliar scenes such as those taken from airplanes, as well as such plausible inventions as an electric cannon and television. The 1916 version of *20,000 Leagues Under the Sea* was the first major production to contain scenes actually filmed underwater, one of them featuring an artificial octopus.

By the 1920s a different vein of fantasy had developed in Germany: the somber psychological melodrama exemplified by Otto Rippert's *Homunculus* (about an artificial man) and Wiene's *Cabinet of Dr. Caligari*. Fritz Lang's *Metropolis* (1926) united this somber fantasy with the more spectacular kind described above. Because of Lang's reputation, the scale of the production (it was the most costly film yet made in Germany), and the impressive futurism of the sets and models, *Metropolis* was subjected to a serious critical scrutiny that was unprecedented for a fantasy film. While most critics praised its visual and lyrical power, few had kind words for its plot or for its conception of a future society. H. G. Wells declared that *Metropolis* would grievously disappoint the vast audiences who were eager to see what a city of a hundred years in the future might be like, and suggested that a rational film on the subject could and should be made. This, as it turned out, was an undertaking that Wells himself was to attempt.

Before then, however, Lang made another film about the future: *Die Frau im Mond* (*Woman in the Moon*, 1929). Here, for the first time, an experimental scientist was engaged as technical adviser on a fictional film: the design of the moon rocket and the procedures of its launching reflect the ideas of rocket pioneer Hermann Oberth. Like *A Trip to the Moon, Die Frau im Mond* is a Space Machine carrying the audience through four stages—preparation, launching, flight, and landing—into the unknown. Excerpts from the script** show how Lang, in attempting to make this journey seem real, depended on scientific plausibility most in the early stages; later he turned to more dramatic means, such as the obsessive excitement of the old professor and the mounting agoraphobia of the engineer. Partly because of the historical importance of the early scenes, most critics have found the later scenes anticlimactic. Nevertheless, the film is also important because it tries to fuse two different strains of fantasy, one based on science and the other on human emotions, into a single new experience.

What *Die Frau im Mond* attempted in space, *Things to Come* (1936) set out to do in time. Wells presented his vision not only of a future city, but also of the steps by which man would arrive there. Once again there are four stages—war, anarchy, reconstruction, and a new society**—leading the audience from the known into the unknown. Like *Metropolis, Things to Come* was a huge production (the most costly film yet made in Britain), and it was subjected to heavy criticism. Most critics found fault, justifiably, with its picture of an ideal society; the *Journal of the British Interplanetary Society* assailed its scientific inaccuracy.** Yet for other critics, like Elizabeth Bowen,** the sweep of the action from present to future and the cogency of *Things to Come* as a filmic experience overrode any such objections.

Things to Come stands out as an exception among the fantasy films of the 1930s and early '40s. In this depression era, most films were content with imagination on a much more local and personal scale. To the general public, science meant more and bigger machines and engineering rather than any earthshaking discovery. Even when spectacular technology did appear in films—such as *F.P.1. Does Not Answer* (1932) with its mid-ocean airport, or *Transatlantic Tunnel* (1933)—its effects were limited in scope compared to the moon flights of *Die Frau im Mond* and *Things to Come*. Most fantasy films revolved around an individual. In Abel Gance's *La Fin du Monde* (1931) the cataclysmic passage of a comet seems to have been wished on the world, for its own good, by the Christlike hero. More often the individual was a scientist, working in isolation, whose invention disrupted the lives of only a small circle of people. The emphasis—as in *Frankenstein, Dr. Jekyll and Mr. Hyde,* and *The Invisible Man*—was on the personal drama, not on what the invention could mean for mankind as a whole. At the same time, some of these films did offer an experience of transformed reality along the lines of Méliès's films: the on-camera metamorphoses of Dr. Jekyll, the lifelike behavior of King Kong, and the contrasts of size in *Dr. Cyclops*. With this last example, ostensibly a horror film about a mad scientist, Ernest Schoedsack clearly relishes the technical challenges it involved,** while Truffaut sees in it an innocent charm that recalls the early days of cinema fantasy.**

Then came World War II, bringing with it the V-2 and the atom bomb, and the general public began to realize that science could drastically affect them, not just in small isolated groups, but by the millions. This was reflected in the realistic fantasies of the 1950s. The scientist working in isolation became more and more rare, and even in films involving only a small group of people there was a clear connection with the world at large: the Arctic community in *The Thing* (1951) must stop the monster from escaping to inhabited regions; *Five* (1951) contains explicit reminders of the billions who did *not* survive World War III.

Along with this change, the United States emerged as the leading producer of realistic fantasies. Before World War II Europe had dominated the field—as it had also dominated the fields of scientific research. Although the transatlantic shift was already under way in the 1930s, the United States had still relied heavily on Europe for its sources (Mary Shelley, Bram Stoker, Robert Louis Stevenson, H. G. Wells) and for its personnel (James Whale and Joe May behind the camera, Boris Karloff, Bela Lugosi, Charles Laughton, Claude Rains in front), while local inspiration had been left to such low-budget quickies as the "Flash Gordon" serials. *Things to Come,* however, with its American director and special-effects team, was prophetic in more than its content.

The new, post–World War II crop of realistic fantasies was unmistakably American in tone and setting, and most of them featured technology as something more pervasive than a single invention or a private laboratory. To describe these films, the term "science fiction" now came into widespread use.

The first important film in this new crop, *Destination Moon* (1950), did reflect post–World War II tensions in its concern for strategic control of the moon; but essentially it was a painstaking picture of what space flight could be like. Heinlein gives a vivid idea of just what pains were taken.** *Destination Moon* went beyond *Die Frau im Mond* in realism by as much as *Die Frau im Mond* had gone beyond *A Trip to the Moon*: it was a fantastic experience made matter-of-fact.

In most films, however, the fantasy was more dramatic, and postwar tension was reflected in global crises and catastrophes. In *The Day the Earth Stood Still* (1951) an alien threatens to destroy mankind if mankind does not stop threatening to destroy itself; most of mankind *is* destroyed in *When Worlds Collide* (1951); *Invasion of the Body Snatchers* (1956) shows mankind being supplanted by an alien life form. Until now, critics had either ignored fantasy films or, like Truffaut with *Dr. Cyclops,* treated them lightly; only with such isolated achievements as *Metropolis* and *Things to Come* had they considered the content worth analyzing. Now there was a change, especially among European critics. *Twentieth Century* magazine denounced *Them!* as a vicious allegory calling for the extermination not of giant ants but of communists;* Pierre Kast praised *The Day the Earth Stood Still* for challenging some of America's sacred cows;** and *Invasion of the Body Snatchers* emerged as a protean film, being interpreted by Ernesto Laura as McCarthyite** and by Guy Braucourt as anti-fascist.**

Some of these films broke away from the usual Hollywood conventions: *Destination Moon* had no "romantic interest," and *The Day the Earth Stood Still* ended on a note that is neither reassuring nor comfortably sad. But others showed less individuality. Arthur C. Clarke expresses his measured disappointment with *When Worlds Collide,* and comments on the difficulty of making a really imaginative SF film;** like Wells after criticizing *Metropolis,* Clarke himself will eventually become involved in the attempt.

By the mid-1950s, most fantasy films had locked themselves into a set of conventions that formed a new subgenre: the monster film. In this, the monster was usually a giant mutation of some existing creature that had been subjected to nuclear radiation; it was first sighted by an individual or a small group whose reports were ridiculed; by the time the authorities did recognize the monster's existence, it had multiplied or in some other way was threatening the whole world; and it was destroyed in a spectacularly violent climax.

Publicized as "science fiction," these monster films appeared with greater frequency than any other type of screen fantasy since the early 1900s. They poured forth not only from Hollywood but also, beginning with *Godzilla* in 1955, from Japan. Richard Hodgens, in a strong indictment of the monster films of the 1950s,** argues that they fixed a narrow and misleading notion of SF in the public mind. Certainly they started a complex debate—which has continued to the present time—over the nature of SF on the screen and its relation to SF writing.

Ado Kyrou, in his appraisal of *The Creeping Unknown* (1955) and *Forbidden Planet* (1956),** finds no basic difference in the ideas of SF films and writing, and also argues that the realism of the filmic image can express those ideas with unusual vigor.

Guy Gauthier finds** that films are at a disadvantage compared to writing in trying to create imaginary yet plausible worlds, so that many of the best attempts are at least partial failures.

Dario Mogno examines both written and filmed SF together,** without adducing any significant differences in the nature of the two media. Like Hodgens, he finds that films have covered only a limited area of the SF represented in writing, but he is skeptical of establishing any clear-cut definition of SF.

The diversity of such views reflects a growing diversity in SF films themselves. From the heyday of the monster film through the present, at least three new trends have emerged, helping to revive the SF film but also making it harder to pin down.

First, Hollywood began to break away from the monster-quickie formula. It resumed the kind of solid, medium-to-high-budget films represented by *Destination Moon* and *War of the Worlds* (1953), and attempted with varying success to inject imagination into such exercises of craftsmanship as *The Time Machine* (1960), *Robinson Crusoe on Mars* (1964), and *The Andromeda Strain* (1971). It is worth comparing the techniques involved in the first of these films, as described in an article from *American Cinematographer,*** with Robert Paul's conception of a Time Machine (page 20). The screen has assimilated Paul's fantasy effects to such an extent that, in a skillful but pedestrian film like *The Time Machine,* they no longer seem very exciting. Not all popular screen SF of the '60s moved in this direction: the low-budget films began to show a greater sophistication. There was now a readiness to use concepts and situations which might baffle spectators not already familiar with SF; some films, indeed, such as *The Human Duplicators* and *The Time Travelers* (both 1964), were crammed with so many disparate ideas that even the filmmakers could not digest them. Other low-budget films, such as *The Day Mars Invaded Earth* (1961), the Japanese *Final War* (1962), and the British *Unearthly Stranger* (1963), displayed a bleakness or ruthlessness which was unusual in any popular fantasy, though such attitudes later became familiar in independent productions such as *Night of the Living Dead* (1968) and *Glen and Randa* (1971).

A second development was the spread of SF films from countries other than the United States, Britain, and Japan. This was a matter not only of production—there had been a sprinkling of SF throughout the film histories of the Soviet Union, Czechoslovakia, Italy, etc. —but also of wider distribution. The launching of the annual Trieste Science Fiction Film Festival in 1963 also helped to draw attention to the diversity of these foreign films. Mogno examines this diversity—of quality as well as style and subject matter—in some detail.**

A third development was the incursion of "mainstream" filmmakers into the SF field. From Stanley Kramer with *On the Beach* (1959) and Losey with *The Damned* (1961), the list extended through such directors as Gregoretti, Godard, Petri, Kubrick, and Resnais. Some of them felt that "science fiction" was too limited a term to describe their work; others set out to bend SF to their personal vision. In making *Fahrenheit 451,* for example, Truffaut records** that he was aiming primarily for lyricism and innocence (qualities similar to those he had perceived and admired in *Dr. Cyclops*).

The first and third of these developments were involved in the landmark SF film of the 1960s, the Kubrick-Clarke *2001: A Space Odyssey*. At the same time, there were parallels with other landmark films of the past. Like *Metropolis* and *Things to Come*, *2001* had a record-size budget. Like *Die Frau im Mond*, it set a precedent for technical accuracy. Like *A Trip to the Moon*, *Die Frau im Mond*, and *Things to Come*, it consisted of a four-stage progression into the unknown—a space-time journey from prehistoric Earth to the moon, to the orbit of Jupiter, and through the Star Gate. Some of the film's technical achievements are examined by Herb A. Lightman.** In different ways, Michel Ciment** and Harry M. Geduld ** assess the importance of *2001* and its place in film history.

Even from this brief survey, it is clear that the SF film has evolved somewhat erratically. It shared a common origin with other branches of the fantasy film, and it has frequently veered close to them by making use of the same technical devices (special effects, artificial settings), dramatic tones (horror, surprise), and even content: as Kyrou points out, SF has taken over many elements of traditional fantasy by giving them some kind of rational basis. However, even if it is impossible to draw a precise line between SF and other kinds of fantasy films, it is not necessary to throw up one's hands, as some critics do, and embrace half of the supernatural.

Broadly speaking, SF films hinge on a change or changes in the world as we know it. The changes may be caused by man or be outside his control. They are intended to have a rational explanation (even if only an inadequate one, or none at all, is offered). In many cases the changes depend on displacements in space or time, which the cinema is particularly well suited to express: man visiting other worlds; aliens visiting the earth; life in the future. The smaller the displacement, the less likely the film is to be accepted as SF: this is obvious when the subject is life in the past, which can be considered as SF only if it predates recorded history; but it also applies to space and to the future (*Lost Horizon* and *Seven Days in May* are at most only on the border line of SF).

Along with these displacements, the SF film also deals with changes in man's environment (either physical or social) and in man himself (either physical or mental), especially those changes which can readily be conveyed in visual terms: catastrophes; new buildings, cities, and machinery; human mutations which affect the bodily appearance; increased mental powers or loss of individuality, which affect bodily behavior. The less widespread, or potentially widespread, the change, the less likely the film is to be accepted as SF: thus *Frankenstein* and the mad doctor movies of the 1930s and '40s, which focus on individual and local changes, are usually excluded.

From this summary of themes it can be seen how SF films differ in emphasis from SF writing. The latter need not gravitate toward large displacements in space and time, or toward manifest changes of any kind; writing can be more abstract and reflective than the film, concentrating less on the processes of change than on its causes and effects. Writing can be richer in ideas; the film, in experience. A viewer familiar with the most sophisticated SF writing can still gain a fresh experience from a simple filmed journey into space.

For many of its critics, however, not only is the SF film less rich in ideas than SF writing, but most of the ideas it does offer are contemptible. The scientific basis of the action is likely to be riddled with errors, while the attitude expressed toward anything strange—creature, behavior, or idea—is usually one of fear and hostility.

To the extent that the SF film has been a form of mass entertainment, fabricated by people who may have worked on a Western the month before and on a thriller the month after, it has undoubtedly stuck close to popular fallacies and prejudices. Of course, the SF film can be defended with the same line of argument that has often been presented in favor of the Western and the thriller: that filmic qualities of vitality and intensity can transcend the limitations of the genre. But there is a more specific defense of the SF film.

Even amid the monster parade of the 1950s, some routine films were able to break with the conventions. In *The Beginning of the End* (1957) the scientists manage to forestall the military's plan of destroying the giant locusts in a nuclear holocaust. In *World Without End* (1956) astronauts who are stranded on an alien earth in the future end up conquering their regrets and building a new life. The fact that *Invasion of the Body Snatchers* could be interpreted as both McCarthyite and anti-fascist suggests an ambivalence in its attitude toward conformity—revulsion tinged with fascination. In different ways, many other SF films are—as Mogno describes the space travelers of *Ikarie XB-1*—"torn between fear of the unknown and the urge to explore": for example, in the mixture of hostility and sympathy shown toward the Creature from the Black Lagoon, or the nostalgia carried in *2001* to the limits of human existence.

This deep-rooted ambivalence can give the SF film a richness that eludes many conscious elaborations of popular genres, such as the sociological thriller or the psychological Western.

In addition, SF films encompass an extraordinary variety of moods and tones. To demonstrate this it is not even necessary to cite any of the mainstream films that lie on the border line of SF (Bergman's *Shame,* Buñuel's *Simon of the Desert,* Kurosawa's *I Live in Fear,* etc.); there are plenty of unequivocal examples. It is true that horror and catastrophe often prevail, but even within these areas there is a world of difference between the Apollonian calm of *La Jetée* and the Dionysian crescendo of *Five Million Years to Earth.* Drawing on the multifarious legacy of Méliès and Lumière, SF films can also be playful (*Paris Qui Dort*), satirical (*Omicron*), or matter-of-fact (*Destination Moon*), evoke a sense of wonder (*The Incredible Shrinking Man, Robinson Crusoe on Mars*) or exhilaration (*Things to Come, 2001*). Their potential for challenging, stimulating, and entertaining seems a long way from being exhausted.

Despite the broad conclusion reached above, the selections in this book make it clear that the nature of the SF film, its relation to SF writing, and its aesthetic value are all matters of continuing debate. The same general point emerges from the survey of SF writers and filmmakers,** which also includes some insights into the practical considerations of SF filmmaking.

Thoughtful and informative studies of the SF film are still rare. Much of the writing that does exist comes either from uncritical fans or from hypercritical devotees of SF literature. The bibliography.** while far from exhaustive, is intended to cover all important books and articles, as well as a number of less satisfactory items which have some use or interest.

The chronology** and filmography** are both necessarily incomplete. The former, however, suggests various points at which the relation between the development of the SF film and other historical events might be explored in detail. The filmography includes not only the major films mentioned in the book but also a selection of less well-known ones that demonstrate the variety and vitality of the genre.

Chronology[1]

1895 Lumière brothers' first films, including *Charcuterie mécanique* (a fantastic machine).
 Roentgen discovers X–rays.

1895–1901 H. G. Wells publishes his best-known SF novels: *The Time Machine* (1895), *The Island of Dr. Moreau* (1896), *The Invisible Man* (1897), *War of the Worlds* (1898), *First Men on the Moon* (1901).

1895 Robert W. Paul, inspired by Wells's novel, plans a cinematographic Time Machine.

1896–1900 Georges Méliès begins making films and develops new techniques for producing fantastic effects.
 Various attempts to synchronize film and phonograph records.

1900 Zeppelin's first rigid airship.
 Planck's quantum theory.
 Freud's *The Interpretation of Dreams*.

1901 Ferdinand Zecca's *Conquest of the Air* (a submarinelike flying machine).

1902 Méliès's *A Trip to the Moon*.
 Pavlov begins his experiments on conditioning dogs.

1903 Martin Duncan's "Invisible World" series of nature films (close-ups and microscopic scenes).
 The Wright brothers' first airplane flights.

1905 Jules Verne dies.
 Einstein's special theory of relativity. (His general theory followed in 1916.)

1906–7 Edwin S. Porter and Stuart Blackton use stop motion to animate objects.

[1] Important dates in the development of the science fiction film from 1895 to the present, together with a selection of relevant events in world history and technology.

1908   Émile Cohl produces the first animated drawings.
            First filming from an airplane (Félix Mesguich with Wilbur Wright).

1909   Walter Booth's *Battle in the Clouds*.
            Peary reaches the North Pole.

1910   Jean Durand's *Onésime Horloger* (undercranking to speed up time).

1911   Méliès's *Conquest of the Pole*.
            Griffith's *Man's Genesis* (a prehistoric drama).

1912   Edgar Rice Burroughs's first Martian novel, *Under the Moons of Mars*.

1913   Henry Ford introduces the assembly-line system of auto production.

1914–18   World War I. The acceleration of technical developments (tanks, long-distance artillery, poison gas, etc.) is reflected in such films as Feuillade's *Fantômas* and *Les Vampires*.

1915   Paul Wegener's *The Golem* (foreshadowing the android, or artificial human being).

1916   Stuart Paton's *20,000 Leagues Under the Sea* (first extensive underwater photography).

1917   Forest Holger-Madsen's *Himmelskibet* (a trip to Mars).
            The Bolshevik Revolution in Russia.

1919   First transatlantic airplane flights.
            Robert Goddard begins his rocket experiments.

1920   Karel Čapek's *R.U.R.* (introducing the term "robot").
            First regular radio broadcasts (U. S.).

1923   René Clair's *Paris Qui Dort*.

1924   Yakov Protazanov's *Aelita* (a Bolshevik revolution on Mars).

1925   *The Lost World* (animated models of prehistoric monsters).

1926   Fritz Lang's *Metropolis* (first extensive vision of the future).
                    Hugo Gernsback launches *Amazing Stories* (first magazine specializing in what was to be known as SF).

1927   *The Jazz Singer* opens the era of sound films.

1929   Fritz Lang's *Frau im Mond* (first space travel film based on scientific ideas. Hermann Oberth was technical adviser).
                    Gernsback coins the term "science fiction."

1931   Gance's *La Fin du Monde* (based on a scientific romance by astronomer Camille Flammarion).
            Whale's *Frankenstein* (paves the way for the "mad scientist" cycle).

1932	*F.P.1. Does Not Answer* (first of several German films based on technological anticipation).
1933	Wells's book, *The Shape of Things to Come.*
	Film versions of Wells's *The Island of Dr. Moreau* (*The Island of Lost Souls*) and *The Invisible Man.*
	King Kong (extensive use of animated models).
1935	First three-strip Technicolor feature (Mamoulian's *Becky Sharp*).
1936	The Korda-Menzies-Wells *Things to Come.*
	Flash Gordon (first of many "space opera" serials).
	First prefrontal lobotomy.
	First regular TV broadcasts (Britain).
1938	The Orson Welles-Howard Koch "War of the Worlds" radio broadcast.
1939	Norman McLaren experiments with synthetic film music—artificially created sound tracks.
1939–45	World War II. Various technological developments, such as radar and jet propulsion. In addition:
1944	The V-2 rocket bomb;
1945	The atom bomb.
	First modern digital computers.
1947	First modern report of a UFO sighting (a popular theme in SF films in the 1950s).
1949	TV production of *The Time Machine* (Britain)
	George Orwell's *Nineteen Eighty-Four.*
1950	*Destination Moon* (first SF film in color; first script by a SF writer—Robert Heinlein—since *Things to Come*).
	Arthur C. Clarke's story, "The Sentinel."
	First SF series on TV ("Captain Video").
1951	*The Thing* (first of the "creature" cycle).
1953	First films in CinemaScope; in Eastmancolor (supplanting the cumbersome three-strip Technicolor); and in 3D.
	It Came from Outer Space (first SF film in 3D).
	Ray Bradbury's *Fahrenheit 451.*
1955	*Godzilla* (Japan enters the scene).
	TV version of *1984* (Britain).
	First nuclear-powered submarine.
1956	*Forbidden Planet* (first SF film in CinemaScope and color; electronic-music score).
	First use of videotape.

1957	The Soviet Union launches Sputnik I, the first artificial earth satellite.
1960s	Development of lasers.

Experimental filmmakers approach the SF field, either through technique (the computer-generated films of the Whitney brothers) or through content (Jordan Belson's *Reentry*, 1964).

"Serious" filmmakers again enter the SF field: Losey with *The Damned* (1961), Godard with *Alphaville* (1965), etc.

1963	First annual SF film festival in Trieste.

Czechoslovakia's *Ikarie XB-1* (East Europe enters the scene).

"Outer Limits" series on TV.

1968	Kubrick's *2001: A Space Odyssey* (multimillion-dollar budget; computer-planned special effects; collaboration of a leading SF author).
1969	Astronauts walk on the moon.
1972	Pioneer 10 launched to fly past Jupiter and leave the solar system.

BEGINNINGS:
1895–1940s

From "Paul and 'The Time Machine'"
by TERRY RAMSAYE

. . . [Robert W.] Paul's attention was arrested by a conspicuous piece of fiction entitled *The Time Machine,* which appeared in 1895. There was a striking relation between the fancy of the story and the fact of the motion picture. The author of this story was H. G. Wells, a science teacher who had turned from the classroom and lecture platform to fiction for his expression. . . .

In this story Paul saw an opportunity to use the special properties of the motion picture in a new and perhaps especially effective method of narration. He wrote to Wells, who went to confer with Paul at his laboratory at 44 Hatton Garden.

A reading of *The Time Machine,* even now, leaves one with a strong impression that the story was born of the direct suggestion of the behavior of a motion-picture film. Wells, in a letter to the writer in 1924, said he was unable to remember details of the relation. But the evidence is such that if the story was not evolved directly from the experience of seeing the Kinetoscope, it was indeed an amazing coincidence.

The Time Machine is a fanciful tale of the adventures of a physicist who built a machine which could travel in time just as an airplane travels in space. The Time Traveler tells his story in the first person. In the third chapter of the Wells story he says:

> I drew a breath, set my teeth, gripped the starting lever with both my hands, and went off with a thud. The laboratory got hazy and went dark. Mrs. Wachett came in, and walked, appar-

From "Paul and 'The Time Machine,'" chapter 12 of A Million and One Nights *by Terry Ramsaye. New York: Simon and Schuster, Inc., 1926; London: Frank Cass Co., Limited, 1954, pp. 152–61. Copyright © 1926 by Simon and Schuster, Inc. Reprinted by permission of Simon and Schuster, Inc., and Frank Cass Co., Limited.*

ently without seeing me, toward the garden door. I suppose it took her a minute or so to traverse the place, but to me she seemed to shoot across the room like a rocket.

In that paragraph one does not have to stretch his fancy to see what must be taken as the motion-picture influence at the bottom of Wells's concept. The operation of the Time Traveler was very like the starting of the peep show Kinetoscope, and the optical effect experienced by the fictional adventurer was identical with that experienced in viewing a speeding film.

But even more strongly is the motion-picture character of the *Time Machine* idea evidenced in Wells's chapter thirteen, where the Time Traveler, nearing the end of his narrative, recites:

I saw one little thing that seemed odd to me. I think I have told you that when I set out, before my velocity became very high, Mrs. Wachett had walked across the room, traveling, it seemed to me, like a rocket. As I returned, I passed again across the minute when she traversed the laboratory. But now every motion appeared to be the direct inverse of her previous one. The door at the lower end opened and she glided quietly up the laboratory, back foremost, and disappeared behind the door by which she had previously entered.

This paragraph details precisely the effect of running a film backward with consequent exact reversal of the action. It is hard to believe that Wells did not take his notion directly from the peep show film. One of the earliest novelty effects sought in the Kinetoscope in the days when it was enjoying scientific attention was in exactly this sort of reversal of commonplace bits of action. It continues today, a somewhat hackneyed bit of trick camera work. In the early days we saw runners backing up at high speed and backing locomotives swallowing their smoke in reverse gear. Nowadays we see Venuses in half-piece bathing suits spring from the pool and retrace the parabola of the dive to alight on the springboard. Such is the progress of art.

Returning to Wells, there is additional evidence of the motion-picture root of the *Time Machine* idea in that he stresses the picture-reversal effect in the phrase: "she glided quietly." Wells seems to have been thinking in terms of the picture exclusively. He, for the moment, ignored the fact that his Time Traveler in recrossing a moment of time should have experienced the sounds as well as the sights of that moment, both reversed. Mrs. Wachett might have just as well also been heard backing up and closing the door. The thing had already been done in experimental reversals of the phonograph. It would seem pretty definite that the Time Traveler was all eyes and the story all motion picture.

Out of the author-scientist collaborations in Hatton Garden came a screen project to materialize the human wish to live in the Past, Present, and Future all at once. It is all set forth in clear terms in a British patent application, No. 19984, drawn up by Paul under date of October 24, 1895, reading:

A Novel Form of Exhibition or Entertainment, Means for Presenting the Same

My invention consists of a novel form of exhibition whereby the spectators have presented to their view scenes which are supposed to occur in the future or past, while they are given the sensation of voyaging upon a machine through time, and means for presenting these scenes simultaneously and in conjunction with the production of the sensations by the mechanism described below, or its equivalent.

The mechanism I employ consists of a platform, or platforms, each of which contain a suitable number of spectators and which may be enclosed at the sides after the spectators have taken their places, leaving a convenient opening towards which the latter face, and which is directed towards a screen upon which the views are presented.

In order to create the impression of traveling, each platform may be suspended from cranks in shafts above the platform, which may be driven by an engine or other convenient source of power. These cranks may be so placed as to impart to the platform a gentle rocking motion, and may also be employed to cause the platform to travel bodily forward through a short space, when desired, or I may substitute for this portion of the mechanism similar shafts below the platforms, provided with cranks or cams, or worms keyed eccentrically on the shaft, or wheels gearing in racks attached to the underside of the platform or otherwise.

Simultaneously with the forward propulsion of the platform, I may arrange a current of air to be blown over it, either by fans attached to the sides of the platform, and intended to represent to the spectators the means of propulsion, or by a separate blower driven from the engine and arranged to throw a regulated blast over each of the platforms.

After the starting of the mechanism, and a suitable period having elapsed, representing, say, a certain number of centuries, during which the platforms may be in darkness, or in alternations of darkness and dim light, the mechanism may be slowed and a pause made at a given epoch, on which the scene upon the screen will come gradually into view of the spectators, increasing in size and distinctness from a small vista, until the figures, etc., may appear lifelike if desired.

In order to produce a realistic effect, I prefer to use for the projection of the scene upon the screen, a number of powerful lanterns, throwing the respective portions of the picture, which may be composed of,

(1) A hypothetical landscape, containing also the representations of the inanimate objects in the scene.

(2) A slide, or slides, which may be traversed horizontally or vertically and contain representations of objects such as a navigable balloon etc., which is required to traverse the scene.

(3) Slides or films, representing in successive instantaneous photographs, after the manner of the Kinetoscope, the living persons or creatures in their natural motions. The films or slides are prepared with the aid of the kinetograph or special camera, from made-up characters performing on a stage, with or without a suitable background blending with the main landscape.

The mechanism may be similar to that used in the Kinetoscope, but I prefer to arrange the film to travel intermittently instead of continuously and to cut off the light only during the rapid displacement of the film as one picture succeeds another, as by this means less light is wasted than in the case when the light is cut off for the greater portion of the time, as in the ordinary Kinetoscope mechanism.

(4) Changeable coloured, darkened, or perforated slides may be used to produce the effect on the scene of sunlight, darkness, moonlight, rain, etc.

In order to enable the scenes to be gradually enlarged to a definite amount, I may mount these lanterns on suitable carriages or trollies, upon rails provided with stops or marks, so as to approach to or recede from the screen a definite distance, and to enable a dissolving effect to be obtained, the lantern may be fitted with the usual mechanism. In order to increase the realistic effect I may arrange that after a certain number of scenes from a hypothetical future have been presented to the spectators, they may be allowed to step from the platforms, and be conducted through grounds or buildings arranged to represent exactly one of the epochs through which the spectator is supposed to be traveling.

After the last scene is presented I prefer to arrange that the spectators should be given the sensation of voyaging backward from the last epoch to the present, or the present epoch may be supposed to have been accidentally passed, and a past scene represented on the machine coming to a standstill, after which the impression of traveling forward again to the present epoch may be given, and the rearrival notified by the representation on the screen of the place at which the exhibition is held, or of some well-known building which by the movement forward of the lantern can be made to increase gradually in size as if approaching the spectator.

Robt. W. Paul

Paul, inspired by Wells's story, in this document of three decades ago exactly anticipated the photoplay, which was not to be born yet for many a year.

It was, viewed from the easy facility of the slowly evolved screen technique of today, a clumsy collection of mechanical expedients. He did not and could not know then that everything sought by way of revolving stages, combined stereopticons, projection machines, scenic settings, masked seating sections, and platform rocking devices to simulate travel motion, would one day be done entirely on the screen. The photoplay of today moves backward and forward through Time with facile miracle from the Present into the Past and Future by the cutback, flashback, and vision scenes. The Paul patent notion of sliding projection machines to enlarge or diminish the size of the picture is executed by the camera of today while the projector stands still in its theater booth. Most amazingly, too, Paul and Wells in 1895 plainly had the idea of not only the cutback and close-up but also the fade-in and fade-out, the overlap-dissolving of scenes into each other, and all of the supplemental tonal effects of sunshine, fog, rain, moonlight, and the like, now common to the screen drama.

Many years of reading Wells's works have rather accustomed us to thinking of him as the forecaster of most of the scientific wonders which have become commonplaces of civilization, as for instance the airplane. But even that is no preparation for the surprising discovery in this long forgotten patent application that Wells and Paul forecast something infinitely more complex than any machine—no less than a whole art form.

The Wells-Paul feat of 1895 surpasses even that remarkable antici-pation by which Savinien Cyrano de Bergerac completely described the phonograph, two centuries before its invention, in his *Histoire Comique des États et Empires de la Lune* published in 1656, the year after his death in Paris.

The anticipations of the phonograph by de Bergerac in the mid-dle of the seventeenth century and of the screen drama in the end of the nineteenth are given still more interest when we realize that these two desires of sight and sound were fused in the one mind of Edison, and that through his single agency they were both material-ized. The line between Art and Science is narrow indeed.

But the Wells-Paul idea, embodied in the patent application, con-tained gropings for a greater and new liberty for art. It sought to liberate the spectator from the instant of Now. The Now to which our consciousness is chained is but a mathematical point of no di-mensions traveling ever forward, describing the line which extends behind us as the Past and ahead of us as the Future.

The same impulse of cosmic adventure which has colored Wells's writing feats of fancy in tales of other worlds and of hypothetical ages was at work here. He wanted free range to lead his audiences at will back and forth along the infinite hyperdimensional line of Time. It was a plan to give the spectator possession, on equal terms, of Was and To Be along with Is. The motion picture was to cut away the hampering fog of the complex sequence of tenses of thought, just as it was to cut back to reality through the misty attenuations of language.

This motion-picture Time-machine idea was artistically at one with Ouspensky's mathematically mysterious philosophy and Ein-stein's philosophically mysterious mathematics. It was a promise of a more concrete application of their remote intellectual abstractions. The author and the philosopher alike often in their flights come beating against the walls of Space and Time. They are just expres-sions of the human wish to be liberated from the cage of the eternal Now.

Way back in the early 1870s Nicolas Camille Flammarion, student of stars and dreamer of dreams, in France, wrote a scientific fantasy tale embodying related concepts, concerning the adventures of an interstellar race, masters of Time and Space. Flammarion's story was widely translated and circulated. In the United States, by coinci-dence, two editions were published in the 1890s just before the birth of the motion picture. The peculiar possibilities of the motion picture's ability to petrify and preserve moments of fleeting time were here and there recognized even in the earliest days of the peep show. Witness the following fragment of an editorial from the *St. Louis Post Dispatch*:

KINETOSCOPE MARVELS

The Kinetoscope, we are told, has recently been made to run backward, and the effects of this way of running it are truly marvelous. In his remarkable romance, *Lumen,* the imaginative French astronomer, Flammarion, conceives of spiritual beings, who, by traveling forward on a ray of light, see, with the keen vision of the spirit, all that ray of light carried from the beginning of creation. By reversing the process and traveling in the contrary direction, they witness the events of history reversed, so that men appear to be rising from the grave, growing young and finally disappearing in the process of birth.

It now seems that the Kinetoscope is to make this wondrous vision possible to us. Already, by allowing it to turn backward, the actions can be seen in reverse order. The effect is said to be almost miraculous. In the process of eating, food is taken from the mouth and placed on the plate.

It has taken the motion picture more than a quarter of a century to grow from the Edison Kinetoscope into the photoplay's modern approximation of the *Time Machine* and the Paul-Wells concept of 1895!

Wells was the first writer, in other words the first professional re-creator of events, to come into contact with the motion picture. This circumstance led nearly to the attainment, at a single stroke, of the photoplay construction which has since come only by tedious evolution.

No writer or dramatist has since made so bold a gesture with reference to the screen as resulted from this tentative joining of Paul's invention and Wells's fancy. They were hampered by no precedent or built-up tradition of the screen industry, such as has affected the thought of every writer or dramatist of subsequent connection with the art. When, more than a decade later, the screen reached for the aid of the writing craft, it had established an audience and precedents of practice which did not permit the scenario writer to be a free agent of expression. The project of 1895 conceived the motion picture as a tool and servant in the business of story telling, while the writers who came in after the lapse of years were to be the tools and servants of the then intrenched motion-picture business.

The actual processes of the evolution which was to realize some measure of this early vision did not well begin until some thirteen years later, in 1908, when D. W. Griffith began to assemble the mechanical and optical properties of the motion picture into a new dramatic technique peculiar to the screen. . . .

From "Méliès"
by MAURICE BESSY

Méliès was a less prolific filmmaker than many people first thought. Between 1895 and 1910 he produced an estimated 685 films. In terms of footage, that amounts to less than a year's output of Griffith or Feuillade. It totals 120,000 feet, or 25 hours of running time, which works out to a yearly average of 75 minutes or the equivalent of one full-length feature.

Méliès's achievement is found not so much in quantity as in quality, in the extreme care he put into even his slightest films. However, this achievement was not recognized right away. During the last two years of the nineteenth century Méliès had already produced six long films, but his work had not yet made any great impression. His first long film, made in 1899, dealt with the Dreyfus case, which at that time had split France in two. It would be going too far to see this film as evidence of some kind of political commitment. . . . Méliès was above all a showman, and for him world events were pretexts for *tableaux vivants* and for historical reconstructions like those he had already made of the Greek-Turkish War of 1897 and of the Spanish-American war in Cuba and the Philippines the year after. In any case, no one at the time took Méliès's *Dreyfus Case* for anything else: there was no outcry over it, even though certain parts, such as "The Journalists' Battle," were treated in a satirical manner. . . . The first film of this kind which did lead to protests, controversy, and notoriety was *Edward VII's Coronation,* which Méliès made in May 1902 immediately after his other worldwide success, *A Trip to the Moon.*

From "Méliès" by Maurice Bessy, Anthologie du Cinéma, *vol. 2 (Paris: L'Avant-Scène/C.I.B., 1967), pp. 22–27, 44–46. Reprinted by permission of the publisher.*

The *Coronation* had been commissioned by Charles Urban, an American who, having settled in London in 1900, now headed Warwick Film and was the London representative of Méliès's Star Film. What made the film unusual was the fact that the coronation, scheduled for July, was postponed until August 9 because the king was unwell; yet the film itself opened in late June at the Alhambra Music Hall in London and, the following month, at provincial music halls on the Empire Palace circuit. According to the publicity, at least 80,000 francs were spent on the production: Méliès made a special journey to London to prepare the drawings and models necessary for reconstructing the event, and the master of the Westminster Abbey ceremonies went to Montreuil to act as "technical consultant." A singer from the Châtelet Theater played Queen Alexandra and a Montreuil dishwasher played Edward VII; but the king fancied he was actually seeing himself on the screen. One Paris newspaper rose up in arms: in tones of indignant protest *Le Petit Bleu* declared: "England, you have been deceived." Of course, Méliès was not trying to deceive anyone. His *Coronation*, an anticipation rather than a reconstruction of a news event, was typical of the way his whole age viewed the world. The illustrated papers of the time regularly offered reconstructions and anticipations of events based on the memory or imagination of their artists, while a variety of enterprises—such as the Saint Denis, Bonne Nouvelle, and Eden Museums—supplied traveling showmen with waxwork tableaux of the most talked-about crimes and political events of the day.

Shortly before making the *Coronation* Méliès had used a plaster model spouting flour to reconstruct the famous eruption of Mont Pelée, which had destroyed the town of Saint Pierre on Martinique on May 8, 1902. The Moltoni Company, which had specialized in magic lantern projectors and slides long before the invention of cinematography, had distributed its own "newsreel" consisting of painted scenes of "Saint Pierre before, during, and after the eruption." In making the *Coronation,* therefore, Méliès was following the spirit of an age which would not become familiar with newsreels in the modern sense for another ten years.

All the same, the furor over the film made Méliès and his Star Film famous throughout the British Empire and the United States. *A Trip to the Moon* clinched this success. . . . The tricks and artistic effects which he had been perfecting blossomed out in this little

masterpiece, which comprised all of his favorite genres: "the reconstruction or anticipation of real-life events; satire; fantasy; carica-
ture; illusionism."

Méliès himself has told how it took him four months to make this
920-foot film, which has ever since been inseparable from his name.
It cost about 10,000 francs—an unusually high figure for the time
—largely because of the stage machinery involved and the cloth-
and-pasteboard costumes representing the heads, bodies, and legs of
the Selenites or moon men. For these, Méliès himself made the
models out of clay and plaster. The moon, symbolized by a woman
sitting on a crescent, was played by a music-hall singer, Bleuette
Bernon; the stars were chorus girls from the Châtelet Theater; the
men were music-hall singers (Delpierre, Farjaux, Kelm, Brunnet)
and actors from the Cluny Theater, such as Victor André; and the
Selenites were played by acrobats from the Folies-Bergère. The first
prints were sold in France in August and in the United States one
or two months later. The film was copied by Edison, by Lubin in
Philadelphia, and undoubtedly by many others as well, since it was
not copyrighted in the States. That is what prompted Méliès shortly
afterward to set up an office in New York with his brother in charge,
so that he could copyright his films and prevent any further piracy.

Méliès's film was inspired by Jules Verne's *From the Earth to the
Moon* and Wells's *First Men on the Moon*. It departed from the
former, however, in having its Earthmen land on the moon. In
Verne's novel, the space travelers missed their mark and only circled
the moon before returning to earth. Méliès followed Verne's method
of transportation—a shell fired from a gun—but then dreamed up
some original and amusing scenes on and below the surface of the
moon. The second part of the film, with its hawk-headed, lobster-
bodied moon men, was inspired by Wells, whose Earthmen were
captured by a race of Selenites that lived underground and looked
like insects. While Méliès's earlier long films had centered mainly
on theatrical displays, *A Trip to the Moon* marked a real cinematic
breakthrough. . . .

Today, when rockets have reached the moon, when we have seen
detailed views of the moon's surface live on television, when space
travelers have been given heroes' welcomes in Moscow and New
York, a film like Méliès's is bound to seem rather pathetic. However, at the same time as Méliès's imagination is dwarfed by the
great cosmic poetry of real-life space travel, it also becomes more
understandable. For all its naiveté, and for all the quaintness it has

acquired over the years, the film demonstrates the truthfulness of poetic intuition: man dreams only of what has existed, what already exists somewhere, or what will exist one day in the world. Amid the childish spectacle and the trappings of the Châtelet and the Folies-Bergère, Méliès's dream gives an attractive shape, touched with humor, to prophecies that are quite striking in the light of today's discoveries. The film may sometimes be silly, but it is never offensive. We may smile at it, but with sympathy and admiration, not with contempt.

Among the other long films that contributed to Méliès's fame, we should mention *The Impossible Voyage* (1904—1,230 feet); *The Merry Frolics of Satan* (1906—1,455 feet); *The Incendiaries* 1906— 920 feet); *20,000 Leagues Under the Sea* (1907—870 feet); and *New York to Paris by Automobile* (1908—1,245 feet). There were also shorter films such as *The Magic Book* and *The Melomaniac*. Outrageous fantasy, realistic reportage, illusionist tricks, slapstick comedy, and 1900-style baroque are all inextricably mixed together in these films, making them truly representative of the many facets of Méliès's talent.

Both *The Impossible Voyage* and *The Merry Frolics of Satan* are reminiscent of *A Trip to the Moon,* but the fantasy is more frenetic, if not more ingenious, and derives more from traditional myths. In the former, there is a trip to the sun instead of the moon, and the film starts out with the same basic scenes—a convocation of scientists, and an iron foundry where the means of transportation are being manufactured. But the film is packed with more incident.

20,000 Leagues Under the Sea has little to do with Jules Verne's novel, since it takes the form of a dream. When a fisherman falls asleep in his hut, the Queen of the Ocean appears before him. She turns him into a naval captain and places him in command of a submarine, which immediately plunges him into the ocean depths. There are practically no extravagant comic effects in the film; at most, it has a poetic irony. Méliès respects the dreamlike mood, treating the film as an opera or stage fantasy, as he had done earlier with *The Kingdom of the Fairies.* . . . Once again he has created a half-realistic, half-poetic vision of the deeps: clusters of seaweeds and other plants, weird grottoes, huge shells, sea monsters, giant fish and crabs, anemones, coral formations, sea horses, squids, and, of course, mythological denizens: nymphs, mermaids, naiads and other water goddesses. But when these mythological creatures make the fisherman fall headfirst into a huge hollow sponge which closes over him, the film is revealed as a dream: our hero has simply fallen out of bed headfirst into a tub and is struggling with his own fishing nets. . . .

Méliès's stage effects can readily be seen as an essential part of his cinematic imagination. While it is true that most of the tricks he used on the screen were ones he had previously devised for the stage, he nevertheless invented new tricks for the cinema; moreover, he also adapted old ones to such an extent that they became cinematic innovations revealing a thorough mastery of the new medium. The filming of miniaturized dancers, the simultaneous enlarging and shrinking of two characters, fantastic situations such as those in *Gulliver's Travels* (1902), and the creation of underwater scenes by filming through aquariums—these effects among many others could never have been contrived on the stage and were therefore essentially cinematic. . . .

Méliès's artistry went far beyond the invention and adaptation of tricks and illusions. His originality lies in the way he integrated these into coherent screenplays, shaping the cinema into an entertainment and an art. The fact that he conceived the film as a synthesis of everything which led up to it indicates the extent to which he was oriented toward the future. To blame him for basing his films on his prior knowledge and mastery of another medium makes little more sense than blaming television for not rejecting photography and the film, let alone the theater and music, or rocket designers for building on the work of yesterday's physicists and chemists. In art as in science and politics, there is never any creation *ex nihilo:* there are only arrangements of familiar elements into new forms. Today there is no doubt that Méliès belongs among these arrangers.

From THE WOMAN IN THE MOON
by THEA VON HARBOU

1. THE LAUNCHING

A two-stage spacecraft is about to be launched on a 36-hour journey to the moon. On board are old Professor Manfeldt, who first had the idea of searching for gold on the moon; Wolf Helius, organizer of the project; Hans Windegger, engineer; Frieda, his fiancee; and Walter Turner, an observer for the financiers who wish to control the moon's gold. There is also a stowaway, a young boy named Gustav, who has not yet been discovered.

Windegger is talking to Frieda and Helius:

"From the moment of takeoff until reaching the necessary velocity of 11,200 meters per second . . ."

A close-up of the speed indicator dial dissolves to a closer shot of the 11,200 mark.

". . . there will be 8 critical minutes of struggle with acceleration, which has a fatal effect upon the human organism if it exceeds 40 meters per second . . ."

A close-up of the acceleration indicator dial.

Windegger goes on talking as Frieda lies down on her couch.

"After these 8 minutes, during which we will feel as though unbearable loads were pulling our bodies back to earth, we will be the victors in the fight against acceleration . . . or . . ."

Windegger puts his hands to his temples. Helius climbs onto his couch. Windegger continues:

"And if we are not able to stabilize the velocity at 11,200—we will zoom—and zoom—on and on and on . . ."

From The Woman in the Moon, *by Thea von Harbou, as directed by Fritz Lang. Transcribed from the print in the Film Library of the Museum of Modern Art, New York.*

Helius looks at Windegger, who continues:

". . . irrevocably lost in the universe—never, never again back to earth . . ."

Helius says: "Windegger, I will handle the stabilizing lever myself!"

Helius and Windegger look at each other. Windegger slumps onto his couch.

Frieda, lying on her couch in the lower compartment of the rocket, looks up through the hatch at Windegger. She clasps her hands together over her heart.

Windegger looks back at her, and clasps his hands over his heart in the same gesture.

Now there is a view of the rocket from the outside. It looks rather like a large artillery shell and stands in a rectangular tank, its base immersed in water.

A radio announcer stands on a platform, speaking into a battery of microphones.

Searchlights sweep continually across the launching site, lighting up the rocket and the watching crowds.

Mechanical arms that have been holding the rocket swing slowly aside.

More views of the rocket in its tank, the crowds, and the whole launching site, with the searchlights still sweeping over them.

Inside the rocket, Windegger and Helius lie on their couches, waiting.

The clock shows 9:28.

Outside, there is a full moon in the sky.

The clock shows 9:29.

Windegger reaches for the control lever.

"60 seconds to go!"

Views of Frieda, Professor Manfeldt, and Turner on their couches, waiting.

Windegger, with his hand on the lever:

"20 seconds to go—lie quietly—take a deep breath!"

The others waiting.

Windegger: "10 seconds to go!"

"5 seconds to go!"

"4 seconds to go!"

"3 seconds to go!"

"2 seconds to go!"

"1!"

"NOW!"

A close-up of Windegger's hand as he pulls the lever.

Outside, fire boils up in the tank, and the rocket starts to rise.

2. Approaching the Moon

The speed of the rocket has been stabilized, and the travelers have now reached the midpoint of their journey to the moon. When they fetch a bottle of cognac to celebrate, they discover the stowaway Gustav. He is accepted—by Helius and Frieda, at least—as an extra crew member.

Now that weightlessness prevails in the rocket, handles have swung down from the ceilings and "stirrups" have risen from the floors.

In the lower compartment, Gustav walks toward the hatchway, placing his feet one after another in the "stirrups." Then he springs up through the hatchway.

In the upper compartment, Helius sits at a control panel making entries in the log. He turns and grins as Gustav sails up through the hatchway and into the air. Helius stands and moves across to help Gustav down to the floor.

Frieda is trying to pour a glass of cognac for Windegger, but the liquid spills from the bottle and floats as globules in midair. Windegger scoops them into the glass and drinks them.

A close shot of the log, headed "Duration of Flight":

"26 hours 30 minutes—Have entered the gravitational field of the moon.

"33 hours 20 minutes—Have approached to within 9,000 kilometers of the moon."

Professor Manfeldt stands looking out through the port, which is almost filled by the image of the moon.

Further log entries: "34 hours 45 minutes—Through directional blasts, gravitational pull restored on board. Turning spaceship in order to prevent a premature crash on the moon, by means of braking blasts."

Now only part of the moon can be seen through the port.

The log again: "35 hours 25 minutes—Are about to reach the far side of the moon. Earth visible only as a setting star."

Manfeldt, Turner, Frieda, and Windegger stand at the port, looking out. Windegger's arm is over Frieda's shoulder.

The cratered surface of the moon appears to rotate beneath them. In the distance, the disk of the earth begins to sink below the lunar horizon.

Frieda clasps her hands together.

The earth sinks out of sight.

Windegger takes his arm from Frieda's shoulder and steps back from the port, his face fixed in a horrified stare. Frieda puts her arms around his neck:

"We will see it again, Hans . . . we will see it again!"

But Windegger does not relax.

Manfeldt and Turner are still looking out of the port. Manfeldt says, eagerly:

"And when will we finally land?"

Windegger: "If there is one spark of reason left in us, we will not land at all!"

From the Filmscript of
THINGS TO COME
by H. G. WELLS

THE UNENDING WAR

. . . A desolate heath. Something burning far away. A sheet of decaying newspaper is fluttering in the wind. It catches on a thorn and as the wind tears at it the audience has time to read the ill-printed sheet of coarse paper:

Britons Bulletin

September 21, 1966. Price Four Pounds Sterling.

"Hold on. Victory is coming. The enemy is near the breaking point. . . ."

The wind tears the scrap of paper to pieces.

Here follows some still and desolate scene to suggest and symbolize our contemporary civilization shattered to its foundations. The exact scene to be chosen could best be left to the imagination and invention and facilities of the model-maker. It might even be different in the American, continental, or British version of the film. *One* of the following scenes will give all the effects needed.

The Tower Bridge of London in ruins. No signs of human life. Sea gulls and crows. The Thames, partly blocked with debris, has overflowed its damaged banks.

The Eiffel Tower, prostrate. The same desolation and ruin.

Brooklyn Bridge destroyed. The tangle of cables in the water. Shipping sunk in the harbor. New York, ruined, in the background.

A sunken liner at the bottom of the sea.

From Things to Come *by H. G. Wells, 1935. Reprinted by permission of the Estate of H. G. Wells.*

A pleasure sea front, Palm Beach or the Lido, Blackpool or Coney Island, in complete and final ruin. A few wild dogs wander through the desolation.

Oxford University in ruins and the Bodleian Library scattered amidst the wreckage.

EVERYTOWN UNDER A PATRIOT CHIEF

. . . The throbbing of an aeroplane very far away becomes faintly audible. Close-up of Gordon's face.

Gordon: "It's a lost skill. It is a dream of the past."

His face changes as the beating of the airplane dawns on his consciousness. He is puzzled. Then his face changes. He looks up in the sky. He points silently.

The whole group is shown. All are staring upward.

Wadsky and the market people, the general crowd in the background, are all becoming aware of the airplane. The aeroplane is seen circling in the sky. This has to be the first *novel* aeroplane seen in the film. It is to be a small new 1970 type. Its wings curve back like a swallow's. It must not be big and impressive like the gas bomber which presently arrives, but it must be "different."

People run out of houses. Everybody staring skywards. Running, shouting—the excitement grows.

Gordon, deeply moved. He addresses Mary. "There it is—you were right—a plane once more! He's shutting off—he's coming down."

The eye of the crowd follows the plane and indicates it is circling down to a descent.

The Boss is the first to become active. "What's all this? Have they got aeroplanes before us? And you tell me we can't fly any more! While we have been—fumbling, they have been active. Here, some of you, find out who this is and what it means! *You* (to one of his guards), you go, and *you* (to another). There was only one man in it. Hold him."

The Boss is a centre of activity.

Boss: "Send for Simon Burton. Get me Simon."

A sly-looking individual, the right-hand man of the Boss, appears from the direction of the Town Hall and hurries up to his chief.

The camera shows Gordon and Mary standing a little aloof, perplexed, full of strange hope, at this wonderful break in the routines of Everytown. Then it returns to Roxana. She watches the Boss and his proceedings with the skeptical criticism of a woman who knows a man too well. Then her mind returns to Mary and she looks for her and discovers Gordon also. She comes across to them.

Roxana to Gordon: "What do you know about it? Do you know anything of this? Who is that man in the air?

Gordon speaks half to himself and half to Roxana and Mary. "It was something *new*. It was a *new* machine. Somewhere they can still make new machines. I didn't dream it was still possible."

Roxana: "But *who* is the man? How does he *dare* come here?"

Close-up of her face as she surveys Everytown and realizes that after all it is not the whole world. Her eyes return to the Boss who is still rather uncertain how to meet this new occasion.

Boss: "Fetch him to the Town Hall. Guard his machine and bring him to me there."

The camera returns to Gordon and Mary.

Gordon: "Come along, Mary. I must see that machine." . . .

RECONSTRUCTION

The object of this part is to bridge, as rapidly and vigorously as possible, the transition from the year 1970 to the year 2036. An age of enormous mechanical and industrial energy has to be suggested by a few moments of picture and music. The music should begin with a monstrous clangor and come down to a smoother and smoother rhythm as efficiency prevails over stress. The shots dissolve rapidly on to one another, and are bridged with enigmatic and eccentric mechanical movements. The small figures of men move among the monstrosities of mechanism, more and more dwarfed by their accumulating intensity.

An explosive blast fills the screen. The smoke clears, and the work of the engineers of this new age looms upon us. First, there is a great clearance of old material and a preparation for new structures. Gigantic cranes swing across the screen. Old ruined steel frameworks are torn down. Shots are given of the clearing up of old buildings and ruins.

Then come shots suggesting experiment, design, and the making of new materials. A huge power station and machine details are shown. Digging machines are seen making a gigantic excavation. Conveyer belts carry away the debris. Stress is laid on the work of excavation because the Everytown of the year 2036 will be dug into the hills. It will not be a skyscraper city.

A chemical factory, with a dark liquid bubbling in giant retorts, works swiftly and smoothly. Masked workers go to and fro. The liquid is poured out into a molding machine that is making walls for new buildings.

The metal scaffolding of the new town is being made and great slabs of wall from the molding machine are placed in position. The lines of the new subterranean city of Everytown begin to appear, bold and colossal.

Swirling river rapids are seen giving place to a deep controlled flow of water as a symbol of material civilization gaining control of nature.

A fantasia of powerful rotating and swinging forms carried on a broad stream of music concludes this part.

Flash the date A.D. 2036.

A loud querulous voice breaks across the concluding phase of this "Transition" music. "I don't *like* these mechanical triumphs."

The voice is the voice of Theotocopulos, the rebel artist of the new era. His face becomes visible, very big on the screen. He speaks with force and bitterness: "I do not like this machinery. I do not *like* this machinery. All these wheels going round. Everything going so fast and slick. No."

The camera recedes from him until he is seen to be sitting at the foot of a great mass of marble. He is wearing the white overalls of a sculptor and carries a mallet and a chisel.

A second sculptor, a bearded man, comes into the picture. "Well, what can we do about it?"

Theotocopulos, as if he reveals the most obscure secret: "Talk."

The bearded man shrugs his shoulders and grimaces humorously as if towards a third interlocutor in the auditorium.

Theotocopulos explodes: "Talk. Radio is everywhere. *This modern world is full of voices.* I am going to talk all this machinery down."

The Bearded Man: "But will they let you?"

Theotocopulos imperiously: "They'll let me. I shall call my talks *Art and Life.* That sounds harmless enough. And I will *go* for this Brave New World of theirs—tooth and claw."

Flash back to date.
A.D. 2036. . . .

FINALE

An observatory at a high point above Everytown. A telescopic mirror of the night sky showing the cylinder as a very small speck against a starry background. Cabal and Passworthy stand before this mirror.

Cabal: "There! There they go! That faint gleam of light."

Pause.

Passworthy: "I feel—what we have done is—monstrous."

Cabal: "What they have done is magnificent."

Passworthy: "Will they return?"

Cabal: "Yes. And go again. And again—*until* the landing can be made and the moon is conquered. This is only a beginning."

Passworthy: "And if they don't return—my son, and your daughter? What of that, Cabal."

Cabal (with a catch in his voice but resolute): "Then presently—others will go."

Passworthy: "My God! Is there never to be an age of happiness? Is there never to be rest?"

Cabal: "Rest enough for the individual man. Too much of it and too soon, and we call it death. But for MAN no rest and no ending. He must go on—conquest beyond conquest. This little planet and its winds and ways, and all the laws of mind and matter that restrain him. Then the planets about him, and at last out across immensity to the stars. And when he has conquered all the deeps of space and all the mysteries of time—still he will be beginning."

Passworthy: "But we are such little creatures. Poor humanity. So fragile—so weak."

Cabal: "Little animals, eh?"

Passworthy: "Little animals."

Cabal: "If we are no more than animals—we must snatch at our little scraps of happiness and live and suffer and pass, mattering no more—than all the other animals do—or have done." (He points out at the stars). "It is that—or this? All the universe—or nothing. . . . Which shall it be, Passworthy?"

The two men fade out against the starry background until only the stars remain.

The musical finale becomes dominant.

Cabal's voice is heard repeating through the music: "Which shall it be, Passworthy? Which shall it be?"

A louder, stronger voice reverberates through the auditorium: "WHICH SHALL IT BE?"

THE END

THINGS TO COME
ANONYMOUS

During recent months, almost every popular scientific journal in England and America has contained some reference to the film, *Things to Come,* but none has pointed out its outstanding misconception—H. G. Wells actually suggests that the scientific world of 2036 will revert to the fantastic, nineteenth-century, Vernian idea of space travel, that by means of a gun-fired projectile.

A little mathematics soon indicates the absurdity of this scheme. I have no data as to the length of the barrel of the "Space Gun," but for the sake of simplicity, we will assume it to be half a mile. To obtain a muzzle velocity of 7 miles per second—the minimum velocity required by the projectile—would necessitate an acceleration up the barrel of 49 miles per second. Assuming the weight of either of the space travellers as 120 pounds, and using the equation $p = m \cdot t$, we see that the force on either person would be about 435 tons!

Although the film characters are made to say such things as "Adjust the shock absorbers," "Contract your muscles," etc., I doubt if the ingenious H. G. Wells—or any other science fiction author, for that matter—could devise a method of making the human body resist a "kick" of 435 tons!

Mr. Wells has incorporated into the "Space Gun" scenes of the film an idea which no astronaut has seriously considered since the days of Jules Verne. If the "Man in the Street" is to be introduced to the possibility of space travel via the medium of films—especially films with as much publicity as was given to *Things to Come*—it is up to the writers of them to make sure their facts are reasonably ac-

From The Journal of the British Interplanetary Society, *February 1937. Reprinted by permission of the British Interplanetary Society.*

curate, and not to give the public the idea that modern astronautical societies resemble the Baltimore Gun Club.[1] Play the game, Mr. Wells!

[1] The society responsible for the flight in Jules Verne's story, *From the Earth to the Moon.*

THINGS TO COME
A Critical Appreciation
by ELIZABETH BOWEN

Mr. Wells' *Things to Come* is, above all, spectacular. But it is unlike the run of "spectacle" films, such as Cecil B. de Mille's, with their teeming casts and ultra-gorgeous settings, that excite the eye and stun the imagination and culminate in some monster cataclysm. The technique of *Things to Come* is controlled and quiet, the cast, all things considered, unexpectedly small; the actors being used with such intelligence that not a figure appears without effect. Though the horrors of war, most notably an air raid on an Every-town that is the London of today, appear in the film early, *Things to Come* is memorable not for its use of horror, its power to wring the nerves, but for its command of two important elements: size and rhythm. Detail is used also, with feeling and precision, but dramatic use of detail is not an innovation; it is for its power to present *size* emotionally, to make one feel either an object or an event to be un-precedented, extraordinary, that this film seems to me chiefly re-markable. Except in one or two of the major Russian films (e.g., the shot in *The Fall of St. Petersburg* of the equestrian statue rear-ing over two peasants' tiny figures), I have never seen sheer enor-mousness photographed before. Our feeling for size is odd; it is childish and non-rational; one beholds very large objects with feel-ings of dread and pleasure. Given even the most expert photog-raphy, the dimensions of the screen make the representation of size difficult. The Eiffel Tower photographs like a toy. On the screen, the best models, the most (in their first conception) impressive sets too often appear tame, or suggest trickery. Machines and buildings

From Sight and Sound *5, no. 17 (Spring 1936): 10–12. Reprinted by permission of* Sight and Sound *and the author.*

seldom command the screen, dwarf the actor, or make us feel their majesty; here they do.

Mr. Wells is a romanticist with a vital attitude towards science. He is an artist with a profound mistrust of art. He is a humanitarian and a moralist first of all: his conception of *Things to Come* lacks both the sternness and the frivolity of an artist's. If the film has a "message," it shows that passion wrecks us, that it is fatal to rate too high a person or an illusion. It is as novelist that his touch here seems to me least happy. He oscillates between the heroic and the domestic. The close-ups of personal drama are not telling; the Cabals and the Passworthys gain little by having been particularized. The women could have stayed ciphers; he chose to make them bores. The dialogue beside the impressive action sounds trivial and once or twice grotesque. Colloquially didactic, almost all sentimental, much of the talk is cackle and I wish he had cut it. His imagination, which is gigantic, works visually: all the drama is here implicit in the actors' movements, and in the situations Mr. Wells creates. There should be less talk—more of Mr. Bliss's magnificent music, with its doomful pulse like distant savage drumming, more sirens, chimes, deadly drone of planes, ruined silences of the old world, humming dynamos of the new. Rhetoric, with a loud-speaker-like, impersonal quality, has, it is true, its place here, and there are some fine passages. But in the best sequences sound and images fuse, heightening the rhythm.

Some of the shots are beautiful; significant in the high poetic sense. The film might well be seen for these alone; they woo the imagination instead of bludgeoning it. The door of the festive house thrown open on Christmas evening, above it, the anxious searchlights crossing in the sky—the shadow of deadly planes falling on sunny white cliffs—the child running along the cheerful grassy skyline to the crashed plane exuding fatal gas—the savage Boss holding court among cracking pillars and gaping domes, the mutilated architecture of an extinct world—the march of the New Man, black steely figures, up the grass-grown streets of ruined Everytown—the shots of machinery.

The opening passages of the film are realistic (and consequently, unnerving); the middle is picaresque, with rescues and counterplots. The end seemed pure fantasy; its intention was (at least by me) forgotten in an amused delight of the eye. As the story marches on into the future, ever further from a present that we know as reality, it becomes more abstract. The material, at its outset, is the familiar;

at its close, the unknown: then images have to be at once amazing and possible. In making sets for the future Mr. Vincent Korda had so much scope that he might well have lost his head. He seems to me to have kept it admirably. Size—as I said before—and a kind of inexorability make the *mise-en-scène* of 2036 impressive. The dresses were less good—the padded togas for men, the women's cellophane halos—and came dangerously near the sentimental and tawdry. The most futurelike element in the 2036 sequence was the sound; a sort of sea-shell humming inside the galleried, shadowless white town. But unhappily there was again a good deal of talk. The people of 2036 seem at once smug and null.

Mr. Wells being a moralist, it is futile to quarrel with him on account of aesthetic flaws. If this film fully came off it might knock one flat; it does not fully come off because of a constant conflict between moral and poetic intention. It tries to be too comprehensive; its aims are confused. Mr. Alexander Korda has worked magnificently, but he, too, was perplexed, or allowed himself to be sidetracked. All the same, *Things to Come* is a film that grows in the memory. It should be seen for its rolling boldness, the excellence of its lighting, its naiveté, its drama, and the unforgettable beauty of some of the shots.

Schoedsack Tells of Making
DR. CYCLOPS
ANONYMOUS

Ask Paramount Director Ernest Schoedsack how he made the amazing *Dr. Cyclops* and he'll answer, "With a slide rule and a blueprint."

Astonishingly enough, Schoedsack isn't kidding. That's actually how the picture was made. To be sure, there were the usual photographic tricks—transparencies, split screens, glass shots, and double exposures. These have been used before, but they are new to Technicolor, and *Dr. Cyclops* bears proof that color will have no hampering effect on the mobility of the screen.

When Schoedsack and Producer Dale Van Every started to make the picture they had an artist illustrate every scene in the script. Each individual scene was sketched, illustrating proportionate sizes of the "little people" with Albert Dekker, who plays Cyclops, and with normal objects.

Then the slide rules and blueprints came into being. Each scene was carefully mapped out. Scale drawings showed where every prop, every piece of furniture, every object in the scene was situated. The special effects experts, the cameramen, and Schoedsack worked out formulas to determine the exact spot the camera would be placed, and the exact position each actor would take.

They even figured on how high the lens had to be from the floor, how far the camera was from the player, how far the player from a table, for example, and whether the player had to be standing on a level floor or on a sloping one. All this was necessary to create the "little people."

From American Cinematographer *21, no. 4 (1940): 158. Reprinted by permission of the publisher.*

Hardest job of the filming was to keep Dekker normal in size, while Janice Logan, Thomas Coley, Charles Halton, Victor Kilian, and Frank Yaconelli became small. Dekker was not permitted, at any time, to look like a giant, while the rest of the troop would be considered normal. To keep this illusion always before the audience the "little people" are shown only in relation to known objects.

For example, Dekker is shown sitting in a chair. He is leaning forward, one arm on a table, while he converses with the "little people." Everything is normal in size. A quick cut shows his victims gazing fearfully up at him.

In the scene are the table and the chair with Dekker in it. The audience, adjusting itself to the change, recognizes Dekker as normal, and sees the people as small.

All the movements—walking, running, gesturing—of the little people were slowed down to emphasize the fact that they were small. The sound mixer, with his complicated apparatus, raised the pitch of their voices, for deep, booming voices hardly would issue from such tiny figures.

Even the dialogue was written so that there were no quick questions or answers, permitting space between each line. Every scene was shot with a stop watch, each speech being delivered in a certain number of seconds. Then there was an interval allowed for a reply from the towering Dekker before the "little people" spoke again. . . .

DR. CYCLOPS
by FRANÇOIS TRUFFAUT

Dr. Cyclops is a fascinating film. We are in Peru, where some American Peruologists (?) arrive for heaven knows what purpose. They run afoul of a mean fellow, one of those scientists who put their knowledge to evil use. Having reduced a horse to a height of twelve inches, this doctor—named Cyclops for his moral as well as his physical myopia—plans to subject his guests to the same process. What's more, he's successful, and we see five persons (including a charming girl) reduced to a height of six inches, running around at the mercy of nature, almost gobbled up by a large cat, and hunted down by Dr. Cyclops to be caught with a butterfly net. As you can see, this is all rather out of the ordinary.

This film, with its erratic color, is now ten years old. That is also its mental age. In films of this kind, where the scientists are mad and people get married at the end, there's hardly ever so much as a kiss. A mere squeeze of the arm is enough for a proposal.

It is through these two ideas—the worthlessness of science without a conscience and respect for women—that such grade Z films link up with the great adult cinema of Hitchcock, Renoir, and Rossellini, bypassing the awful middle ground which Jean-Pierre Barrot solemnly calls "the tradition of quality" but which I consider to be the awkward age of the cinema, with all that that implies in the way of low humor and spiteful hypocrisy.

What attracts me to films of fantasy is their revelation of everyday life. The simple beauty of a bare arm, the velvety smoothness of a woman's shoulders or the texture of her dress, the freshness of a knee innocent of any nylon—apart from Hitchcock, Rossellini, and

From Cahiers du Cinéma, *no. 25 (July 1953): 58. Copyright © 1966 by Les Éditions de l'Étoile. Reprinted by permission of Les Éditions de Él'toile and Grove Press, Inc. Translated by William Johnson.*

Renoir (again) only Elmer Clifton, Douglas Sirk, Ida Lupino, and a few others can express these things.

This high regard for women and for the respect due to them is the cinema's most precious possession, in the realm both of ideas and of eroticism.

This extreme reticence and delicacy of feeling remind me of the magazines I read in childhood. From one of them I learned the most beautiful word in the world: the word "idyll."

POPULAR YEARS:
THE 1950s

Shooting
DESTINATION MOON
by ROBERT A. HEINLEIN

"Why don't they make more science fiction movies?"

The answer to any question starting, "Why don't they—" is almost always, "Money."

I arrived in Hollywood with no knowledge of motion-picture production or costs, no experience in writing screenplays, nothing but a yen to write the first Hollywood picture about the first trip to the moon. Lou Schor, an agent who is also a science fiction enthusiast, introduced me to a screenwriter, Alford van Ronkel; between us we turned out a screenplay from one of my space travel stories.

So we were in business—

Uh, not quite. The greatest single production problem is to find someone willing to risk the money. People who have spare millions of dollars do not acquire them by playing angel to science fiction writers with wild ideas.

We were fortunate in meeting George Pal of George Pal Productions, who became infected with the same madness. So we had a producer—*now* we were in business.

Still not quite—producers and financiers are not the same thing. It was nearly a year from the writing of the screenplay until George Pal informed us that he had managed to convince an angel. (How? Hypnosis? Drugs? I'll never know. If I had a million dollars, I would sit on it and shoot the first six science fiction writers who came my way with screenplays.)

From Astounding Science Fiction *July 1950. Copyright* © *1950 by Robert A. Heinlein. Reprinted by permission of the author's agent, Lurton Blassingame.*

Despite those huge Hollywood salaries, money is as hard to get in Hollywood as anywhere. The money men in Hollywood write large checks only when competition leaves them no alternative; they prefer to write small checks, or no checks at all. Even though past the big hurdle of getting the picture financed, money trouble remains with one throughout production; if a solution to a special-effects problem costs thirty thousand dollars but the budget says five thousand dollars, then you have got to think of an equally good five thousand dollars solution—and that's all there is to it.

I mention this because there came a steady stream of non-motion-picture folk who were under the impression that thousand-dollar-a-week salaries were waiting for them in a science fiction picture. The budget said, "No!"

The second biggest hurdle to producing an accurate and convincing science fiction picture is the "Hollywood" frame of mind—in this case, people in authority who either don't know or don't care about scientific correctness and plausibility. Ignorance can be coped with; when a man asks, "What does a rocket have to *push* against, out there in space?" It is possible to explain. On the other hand, if his approach is, "Nobody has ever been to the moon; the audiences won't know the difference," it is impossible to explain anything to him; he does not know and does not want to know.

We had plenty of both sorts of trouble.

That the picture did not end up as a piece of fantasy, having only a comic-book relation to real science fiction, can be attributed almost entirely to the integrity and good taste of Irving Pichel, the director. Mr. Pichel is not a scientist, but he is intelligent and honest. He believed what Mr. [Chesley] Bonestell and I told him and saw to it that what went on the screen was as accurate as budget and ingenuity would permit.

By the time the picture was being shot the entire company—actors, grips, cameramen, office people—became imbued with enthusiasm for producing a picture which would be scientifically acceptable as well as a box office success. Willy Ley's *Rockets and Space Travel* was read by dozens of people in the company. Bonestell and Ley's *Conquest of Space* was published about then and enjoyed a brisk sale among us. Waits between takes were filled by discussions of theory and future prospects of interplanetary travel.

As shooting progressed we began to be deluged with visitors of technical background—guided missiles men, astronomers, rocket engineers, aircraft engineers. The company, seeing that their work was being taken seriously by technical specialists, took pride in turning out an authentic job. There were no more remarks of "What difference does it make?"

Which brings us to the third hurdle—the *technical* difficulties of filming a spaceship picture.

The best way to photograph space flight convincingly would be to raise a few hundred million dollars, get together a scientific and engineering staff of the caliber used to make the A-bomb, take over the facilities of General Electric, White Sands, and Douglas Aircraft, and *build* a spaceship.

Then go along and photograph what happens.

We had to use the second-best method—which meant that every shot, save for a few before takeoff from Earth, had to involve special effects, trick photography, unheard of lighting problems. All this is expensive and causes business managers to grow stomach ulcers. In the ordinary motion picture there may be a scene or two with special effects; this picture had to be *all* special effects, most of them never before tried.

If you have not yet seen the picture, I suggest that you do not read further until after you have seen it; in this case it is more fun to be fooled. Then, if you want to look for special effects, you can go back and see the picture again. (Adv.)

The moon is airless, subject only to one-sixth gravity, bathed in undiluted sunlight, covered with black sky through which shine brilliant stars, undimmed by cloud or smog. It is a place of magnificent distances and towering mountains.

A sound stage is usually about thirty feet high, and perhaps a hundred and fifty feet long. Gravity is Earth normal. It is filled with cigarette smoke, arc light fog, and dust—not to mention more than a hundred technicians.

Problem: to photograph *in a sound stage* men making a rocket landing on the Moon, exploring its endless vistas, moving and jumping under its light gravity. Do this in Technicolor, which adds a sheaf of new problems, not the least of which is the effect of extra hot lights on men wearing spacesuits.

The quick answer is that it can't be done.

A second answer is to go on location, pick a likely stretch of desert, remove by hand all trace of vegetation, and shoot the "real" thing. Wait a minute; how about that black and star-studded sky? Fake it—use special effects. Sorry; once blue sky is on Technicolor emulsion it is there to say. With black and white there are ways, but not with color.

So we are back on the sound stage and we *have* to shoot it there. Vacuum clear atmosphere? No smoking—hard to enforce—high speed on all blowers, be resigned to throwing away some footage, and leave the big doors open—which lets in noise and ruins the sound track. Very well, we must dub in the sound—and up go the costs—but the air *must* be clear.

Low gravity and tremendous leaps—piano wire, of course—but did you ever try to wire a man who is wearing a spacesuit? The wires have to get inside that suit at several points, producing the effect a nail has on a tire, i.e., a man wearing a pressurized suit cannot be suspended on wires. So inflation of suits must be replaced by padding, at least during wired shots. But a padded suit does not wrinkle the same way a pressurized suit does and the difference shows. Furthermore, the zippered openings for the wires can be seen. Still worse, if inflation is to be faked with padding, how are we to show them putting on their suits?

That sobbing in the background comes from the technical adviser —yours truly—who had hoped not only to have authentic pressure suits but had expected to be able to cool the actors under the lights by the expansion of gas from their air bottles. Now they must wear lamb's wool padding and will have no self-contained source of breathing air, a situation roughly equivalent to doing heavy work at noon in desert summer, in a fur coat while wearing a bucket over your head.

Actors are a hardy breed. They did it.

To get around the shortcomings of padded suits we worked in an "establishing scene" in which the suits were shown to be of two parts, an outer chafing suit and an inner pressure suit. This makes sense; deep-sea divers often use chafing suits over their pressure suits, particularly when working around coral. The relationship is that of an automobile tire carcass to the inner tube. The outer part takes the beating and the inner part holds the pressure. It is good engineering and we present this new wrinkle in spacesuits without apology. The first men actually to walk the rugged floor of the Moon and to climb its sharp peaks, will, if they are wise, use the same device.

So we padded for wire tricks and used air pressure at other times. Try to see when and where we switched. I could not tell—and I saw the scenes being shot.

Now for that lunar landscape which has to be compressed into a sound stage—I had selected the crater Aristarchus. Chesley Bonestell did not like Aristarchus; it did not have the shape he wanted, nor the height of crater wall, nor the distance to apparent horizon. Mr. Bonestell knows more about the surface appearance of the Moon than any other living man; he searched around and found one he liked—the crater Harpalus, in high northern latitude, facing the Earth. High latitude was necessary so that the Earth would appear down near the horizon where the camera could see it and still pick up some lunar landscape; northern latitude was preferred so that the Earth would appear in the conventional and recognizable school-room-globe attitude.

Having selected it, Mr. Bonestell made a model of it on his dining room table, using beaver board, plasticine, tissue paper, paint, anything at hand. He then made a pinhole photograph from its center —Wait; let's list the stages:

1. A Mount Wilson observatory photograph.
2. Bonestell's tabletop model.
3. A pinhole panorama.
4. A large blowup.
5. A Bonestell oil painting, in his exact detail, about twenty feet long and two feet high, in perspective as seen from the exit of the rocket, one hundred fifteen feet above the lunar surface.
6. A blown-up photograph, about three feet high, of this painting.
7. A scenic painting, about four feet high, based on this photograph and matching the Bonestell colors, but with the perspective geometrically changed to bring the observer down to the lunar floor.
8. A scenic backing, twenty feet high, to go all around a sound stage, based on the one above, but with the perspective distorted to allow for the fact that sound stages are oblong.
9. A floor for the sound stage, curved up to bring the foreground of the scene into correct perspective with the backing.
10. A second backdrop of black velvet and "stars."

The result . . . looks like a Bonestell painting because it *is* a Bonestell painting—in the same sense that a Michelangelo mural is still the work of the master even though a dozen of the master's pupils may have wielded the brushes.

Every item went through similar stages. I was amazed at the thoroughness of preliminary study made by the art department— Ernest Fegté and Jerry Pycha—before any item was built to be photographed. Take the control room of the spaceship. This compartment was shaped like the frustum of a cone and was located near the nose of spaceship *Luna*. It contained four acceleration couches, instruments and controls of many sorts, an airplane pilot's seat with controls for landing on Earth, radar screens, portholes, and a hatch to the air lock—an incredibly crowded and complicated set. (To the motion-picture business this was merely a "set," a place where actors would be photographed while speaking lines.)

To add to the complications the actors would sometimes read their lines while hanging upside down in midair in this set, or walking up one of its vertical walls. Add that the space was completely enclosed, about as small as an elevator cage, and had to contain a Technicolor sound camera housed in its huge soundproof box—called a "blimp," heaven knows why.

I made some rough sketches. Chesley Bonestell translated these into smooth drawings, adding in his own extensive knowledge of spaceships. The miniature shop made a model which was studied by the director, the art director, and the cameraman, who promptly tore it to bits. It wouldn't do at all; the action could not be photographed, could not even be seen, save by an Arcturian Bug-Eyed Monster with eyes arranged around a spherical 360°.

So the miniature shop made another model, to suit photographic requirements.

So I tore that one apart. I swore that I wouldn't be found dead around a so-called spaceship control room arranged in any such fashion; what were we making? A comic strip?

So the miniature shop made a third model.

And a fourth.

Finally we all were satisfied. The result, as you see it on the screen, is a control room which might very well be used as a pattern for the ship which will actually make the trip some day, provided the ship is intended for a four-man crew. It is a proper piece of economical functional design, which could do what it is meant to do.

But it has the unique virtue that it can be photographed as a motion-picture set.

A writer—a fiction writer, I mean, not a screen writer—is never bothered by such considerations. He can play a dramatic scene inside a barrel quite as well as in Grand Central Station. His mind's eye looks in any direction, at any distance, with no transition troubles and no jerkiness. He can explain anything which is not clear. But in motion pictures the camera has got to *see* what is going on and must see it in such a fashion that the audience is not even aware of the camera, or the illusion is lost. The camera must see

all that it needs to see to achieve a single emotional effect from a
single angle, without bobbing back and forth, or indulging in awkward, ill-timed cuts. This problem is always present in motion-
picture photography; it was simply exceptionally acute in the control
room scenes. To solve it all was a real *tour de force;* the director of
photography, Lionel Lindon, aged several years before we got out
of that electronic Iron Maiden.

In addition to arranging the interior for camera angles it was necessary to get the camera *to* the selected angles—in this enclosed
space. To accomplish this, every panel in the control room was
made removable—"wild" they call it—so that the camera could stick
in its snout and so that lights could be rigged. Top and bottom and
all its sides—it came apart like a piece of Meccano. This meant
building of steel instead of the cheap beaver-board-and-wood frauds
usually photographed in Hollywood. The control room was actually
stronger and heavier than a real spaceship control room would be.
Up went the costs again.

Even with the set entirely "wild" it took much, much longer to
shift from one angle to another angle than it does on a normal
movie set, as those panels had to be bolted and unbolted, heavy
lights had to be rigged and unrigged—and the costs go sky high.
You can figure overhead in a sound stage at about a thousand dollars
an *hour,* so, when in the movie you see the pilot turn his head and
speak to someone, then glance down at his instruments, whereupon
the camera also glances down to let you see what he is talking about,
remember how much time and planning and money it took to let
you glance at the instrument board. This will help to show why
motion-picture theaters sell pop corn to break even—and why science
fiction pictures are not made every day. Realism is confoundedly expensive.

Nor did the costs and the headaches with the control room stop
there. As every reader of *Astounding* knows, when a rocket ship is
not blasting, everything in it floats free—"free fall." Men float
around—which meant piano wires inside that claustrophobic little
closet. It was necessary at one point to show a man floating out from
his acceleration couch and into the center of the room. Very well;
unbolt a panel to let in the wires. Wups! while a spaceship in space
has no "up" or "down," sound stage three on Las Palmas Avenue
in Hollywood certainly does have; supporting wires must run vertically—see Isaac Newton. To float the man out of the tight little

space he was in would require the wires to turn a corner. Now we needed a Hindu fakir capable of the Indian rope trick.

The special effects man, Lee Zavitz, has been doing impossible tricks for years. He turned the entire set, tons of steel, on its side and pulled the actor out in what would normally be a horizontal direction. Easy!

So easy that the art department had to design double gimbals capable of housing the entire set, engineer it, have it built of structural steel, have it assembled inside a sound stage since it was too big to go through the truck doors. Machinery had to be designed and installed to turn the unwieldy thing. Nothing like it had ever been seen in Hollywood, but it did enable a man to float out from a confined space and, later, to walk all around the sides of the control room with "magnetic" boots.

This double-gimbals rig, three stories high, put the control room set high in the air, so the carpenters had to build platforms around it and the camera had to be mounted on a giant boom—one so huge, so fancy, and so expensive that Cecil B. de Mille came over to inspect it. The camera itself had to be mounted in gimbals before it was placed on the boom, so that it might turn with the set— or the other way, for some special effects. This meant removing its soundproof blimp, which meant dubbing the sound track.

("Who cares? It's only money." Don't say that in the presence of the business manager; he's not feeling well.)

This was not the end of the control room tricks. Some of the dodges were obvious, such as making dial needles go around, lights blink on and off, television and radar screens light up—obvious, but tedious and sometimes difficult. Producing the effect of a ship blasting off at six gravities requires something more than sound track of a rocket blast, as the men each weigh over a thousand pounds during blast. Lee Zavitz and his crew built large inflated bladders into each acceleration couch. Whenever the jet was "fired" these bladders would be suddenly deflated and the actors would be "crushed" down into their cushions.

A thousand-pounds weight compresses the man as well as his mattress, which will show, of course, in his features. The makeup man fitted each actor with a thin membrane, glued to his face, to which a yoke could be rigged back of his neck. From the yoke a lever sequence reaching out of the scene permitted the man's features to be drawn back by the "terrible" acceleration. Part of what you see is acting by some fine actors, Dick Wesson, Warner Anderson, Tom Powers, John Archer; part was a Rube Goldberg trick.

The air suddenly escaping from the bladders produced a sound like that of a mournful cow, thus requiring more dubbing of sound track. The air had to be returned to the bladders with equal suddenness when the jet cut off, which required a compressed air system more complicated than that used by a service station.

The sets abounded in compressed air and hydraulic and electrical systems to make various gadgets work—to cycle the air lock doors, to rig out the exit ladder, to make the instrument board work—all designed by Zavitz. Lee Zavitz is the man who "burned Atlanta" in *Gone With the Wind,* forty acres of real fire, hundreds of actors, and not a man hurt. I saw him stumped just once in this film, through no fault of his. He was controlling an explosion following a rocket crash. It was being done full size, out on the Mojave Desert, and the camera angle stretched over miles of real desert. From a jeep back of the camera Zavitz was cueing the special effects by radio. In the middle of the explosions the radio decided to blow a tube— and the action stopped, ruining an afternoon's work. We had to come back and do it over the next day, after a sleepless night of rebuilding by the special-effects crew. Such things are why making motion pictures produces stomach ulcers but not boredom.

The greatest single difficulty we encountered in trying to fake realistically the conditions of space flight was in producing the brilliant starry sky of empty space. In the first place nobody knows what stars look like out in space; it is not even known for sure whether twinkling takes place in the eye or in the atmosphere. There is plausible theory each way. In the second place the eye is incredibly more sensitive than is Technicolor film; the lights had to be brighter than stars to be picked up at all. In the third place, film, whether used at Palomar or in a Technicolor camera, reports a point light source as a circle of light, with diameter dependent on intensity. On that score alone we were whipped as to complete realism; there is no way to avoid the peculiarities inherent in an artificial optical system.

We fiddled around with several dodges and finally settled on automobile headlight bulbs. They can be burned white, if you don't mind burning out a few bulbs; they come in various brightnesses; and they give as near a point source of light as the emulsions can record —more so, in fact. We used nearly two thousand of them, strung on seventy thousand feet of wire.

But we got a red halation around the white lights. This resulted from the fact that Technicolor uses three films for the three primary colors. Two of them are back to back at the focal plane, but the red-sensitive emulsion is a gnat's whisker away, by one emulsion thickness. It had me stumped, but not the head gaffer. He covered each light with a green gelatine screen, a "gel," and the red halation was gone, leaving a satisfactory white light.

The gels melted down oftener than the bulbs burned out; we had to replace them each day at lunch hour and at "wrap up."

There was another acute problem of lighting on the lunar set. As we all know, sunlight on the moon is the harshest of plastic light, of great intensity and all from one direction. There is no blue sky overhead to diffuse the light and fill the shadows. We needed a sound-stage light which would be as intense as that sunlight—a single light.

No such light has ever been developed.

During the war, I had a research project which called for the duplication of sunlight; I can state authoritatively that sunlight has not yet been duplicated. An arc light, screened by Pyrex, is the closest thing to it yet known—but the movies already use arc lights in great numbers, and the largest arc light bulb, the "brute," is not nearly strong enough to light an entire sound stage with sunlight intensity—raw sunlight, beating down on the lunar set would have been equivalent to more than fifteen hundred horsepower. There are no such arc lights.

We traced down several rumors of extremely intense lights. In each case we found either that the light was not sufficiently intense for an entire sound stage, or it was monochromatic—worse than useless for Technicolor.

We got around it by using great banks of brutes, all oriented the same way and screened to produce approximate parallelism. Even with the rafters loaded with the big lights almost past the safety point, it was necessary to use some crosslighting to fill gaps. The surface of the moon had some degree of "fill" in the shadows by reflection from cliff walls and the ground; it is probable that we were forced to fill too much. We used the best that contemporary engineering provides—and next time will gladly use an atomic-powered simulation of the sun's atomic-powered light.

The simulation of raw sunlight was better in the scenes involving men in spacesuits outside the ship in space, as it was not necessary to illuminate an entire sound stage but only two or three human figures; a bank of brutes sufficed and no fill was needed, nor wanted, since there was no surrounding landscape to fill by reflection.

The effect was rather ghostly; the men were lighted as is the Moon in half phase, brilliantly on one side, totally unlighted and indistinguishable from the black sky itself on the other side.

This scene in which men are outside the ship in space involved another special effect—the use of a compressed oxygen bottle as a makeshift rocket motor to rescue a man who has floated free of the ship. The energy stored by compressing gas in a large steel bottle is quite sufficient for the purpose. I checked theory by experiment; opening the valve wide on such a charged bottle gave me a firm shove. The method is the same as that used to propel a toy boat with a CO_2 cartridge from a fizz water bottle—the basic rocket principle.

We had considered using a shotgun, since everyone is familiar with its kick, but we couldn't think of an excuse for taking a shotgun to the Moon. Then we considered using a Very pistol, which has a strong kick and which might well be taken to the Moon for signaling. But it did not *look* convincing and it involved great fire hazard in a sound stage. So we settled on the oxygen bottle, which looked impressive, would work, and would certainly be available in a spaceship.

However, since we were still on Las Palmas Avenue and not in space, it had to be a wire trick, with four men on wires, not to mention the oxygen bottle and several safety lines. That adds up to about thirty-six wires for the heavy objects and dozens of black threads for the safety lines—and all this spaghetti must not show. Each man had to have several "puppeteers" to handle him, by means of heavy welded pipe frames not unlike the cradles used by Tony Sarg for his marionettes, but strong enough for men, not dolls. These in turn had to be handled by block and tackle and overhead traveling cranes. Underneath all was a safety net just to reassure the actors and to keep Lee Zavitz from worrying; our safety factor on each rig was actually in excess of forty, as each wire had a breaking strength of eight hundred pounds. To top it off each man had to wear a cumbersome, welded iron, articulated harness under his spacesuit for attachment of wires. This was about as heavy and uncomfortable as medieval armor.

The setups seemed to take forever. Actors would have to be up in the air on wires for as long as two hours just to shoot a few seconds of film. For ease in handling, the "oxygen bottle" was built of balsa wood and imbedded in it was a small CO_2 bottle of the fire extinguisher type. This produced another headache, as, after a few seconds of use, it would begin to produce carbon dioxide "snow," which fell straight down and ruined the illusion.

But the wires were our real headache. One member of the special-effects crew did nothing all day long but trot around with a thirty-foot pole with a paint-soaked sponge on the end, trying to kill highlights on the wires. Usually he was successful, but we would never know until we saw it on the screen in the daily rushes. When he was not successful, we had to go back and do the whole tedious job over again.

Most of creating the illusion of space travel lay not in such major efforts, but in constant attention to minor details. For example, the crew members are entering the air lock to go outside the ship in free fall. They are wearing "magnetic" boots, so we don't have to wire them at this point. Everything in the air lock is bolted down, so there is nothing to spoil the illusion of no up-and-down. Very well—"Quiet, everybody! Roll 'em!"

"Speed!" answers the sound man.

"Action!"

The actors go to the lockers in which their spacesuits are kept, open them—and the suits are hanging straight down, which puts us back on Las Palmas Avenue! "Hold it! Kill it! Where is Lee Zavitz?"

So the suits are hastily looped up with black thread into a satisfactory "floating" appearance, and we start over.

Such details are ordinarily the business of the script girl who can always be depended on to see to it that a burning cigarette laid down on Monday the third will be exactly the same length when it is picked up on Wednesday the nineteenth. But it is too much to expect a script girl to be a space flight expert. However, by the end of the picture, our script clerk, Cora Palmatier, could pick flaws in the most carefully constructed space yarn. In fact, everybody got into the act and many flaws were corrected not because I spotted them but through the alertness and helpfulness of others of the hundred-odd persons it takes to shoot a scene. Realism is compounded of minor details, most of them easy to handle if noticed. For example, we used a very simple dodge to simulate a Geiger counter—we used a real one.

A mass of background work went into the flight of the spaceship

Luna which appears only indirectly on the screen. Save for the atomic-powered jet, a point which had to be assumed, the rest of the ship and its flight were planned as if the trip actually were to have been made. The mass ratio was correct for the assumed thrust and for what the ship was expected to do. The jet speed was consistent with the mass ratio. The trajectory times and distances were all carefully plotted, so that it was possible to refer to charts and tell just what angle the Earth or the Moon would subtend to the camera at any given instant in the story. This was based on a precise orbit —calculated, not by me, but by your old friend, Dr. Robert S. Richardson of Mount Wilson and Palomar Mountain.

None of these calculations appears on the screen but the results do. The *Luna* took off from Lucerne Valley in California on June 20th at ten minutes to four, zone eight time, with half Moon overhead and the Sun just below the eastern horizon. It blasted for three minutes and fifty seconds and cut off at an altitude of eight hundred seven miles, at escape speed in a forty-six-hour orbit. Few of these data are given the audience—but what the audience sees out the ports is consistent with the above. The time at which they pass the speed of sound, the time at which they burst up into sunlight, the Bonestell backdrops of Los Angeles County and of the western part of the United States, all these things match up. Later, in the approach to the Moon, the same care was used.

Since despite all wishful thinking we are still back on Las Palmas Avenue, much of the effect of taking off from Earth, hurtling through space and landing on the Moon had to be done in miniature. George Pal was known for his "Puppetoons" before he started producing feature pictures; his staff is unquestionably the most skilled in the world in producing three-dimensional animation. John Abbott, director of animation, ate, slept, and dreamed the Moon for months to accomplish the few bits of animation necessary to fill the gaps in the live action. Abbott's work is successful only when it isn't noticed. I'll warrant that you won't notice it, save by logical deduction, i.e., since no one has been to the Moon as yet, the shots showing the approach for landing on the Moon *must* be animation—and they are. Again, in the early part of the picture you will see the *Luna* in Lucerne Valley of the Mojave Desert. You know that the ship is full size for you see men climbing around it, working on it, getting in the elevator of the gantry crane and entering it—and it *is* full size; we trucked it in pieces to the desert and set it up there. Then you will see the gantry crane pull away and the *Luna* blasts off for space.

That *can't* be full size; no one has ever done it.

Try to find the transition point. Even money says you pick a point either too late or too soon.

The *Luna* herself is one hundred fifty feet tall; the table model of her and the miniature gantry crane are watchmaker's dreams. The miniature floodlights mounted on the crane are the size of my little fingertip—and they work. Such animation is done by infinite patience and skill. Twenty-four separate planned and scaled setups are required for each second of animation on the screen. Five minutes of animation took longer to photograph than the eighty minutes of live action.

At one point it seemed that all this planning and effort would come to nothing; the powers-that-be decided that the story was too cold and called in a musical comedy writer to liven it up with—sssh—sex. For a time we had a version of the script which included dude ranches, cowboys, guitars and hillbilly songs on the Moon, a trio of female hepsters singing into a mike, interiors of cocktail lounges, and more of the like, combined with pseudoscientific gimmicks which would have puzzled even Flash Gordon.

It was never shot. That was the wildest detour on the road to the Moon; the fact that the *Luna* got back into orbit can be attributed to the calm insistence of Irving Pichel. But it gives one a chilling notion of what we may expect from time to time.

Somehow, the day came when the last scene had been shot and, despite Hollywood detours, we had made a motion picture of the first trip to the Moon. Irving Pichel said "Print it!" for the last time, and we adjourned to celebrate at a bar the producer had set up in one end of the stage. I tried to assess my personal account sheet—it had cost me eighteen months work, my peace of mind, and almost all of my remaining hair.

Nevertheless, when I saw the "rough cut" of the picture, it seemed to have been worth it.

WHEN WORLDS COLLIDE
Reviewed by A. C. CLARKE

The well-deserved success of *Destination Moon* made the news
that the George Pal—Chesley Bonestell partnership was working on
further interplanetary films all the more welcome. It is with considerable regret that we must record our disappointment with their
second offering, *When Worlds Collide*.

Perhaps one should make clear at once the difference between
the two films. *Destination Moon* was a straight "documentary" of
the first lunar flight. It was not concerned with any other plot elements, was devoid of romance, and the characters were of secondary
importance.

When Worlds Collide, based on the 1932 Balmer and Wylie novel
of the same title, is concerned with a far greater theme—nothing
less than the end of the world and the migration of a few survivors
to another planet. It has a number of well-defined characters and a
good deal of love interest. Yet although the film contains moments
of great excitement and never fails to hold interest, the final effect
is one of anticlimax. This is largely owing to a script of a naiveté
unusual even for Hollywood.

The story is simple enough—a dying sun enters the Solar System
on a course that will eventually cause a collision with Earth. It has
a single planet, and the only hope of mankind is that spaceships can
be constructed in the eight (!) months before the collision, to travel
to the solitary planet of the invading star.

The sequences showing the building of the spaceship are ex-
cellently done and we must give Chesley Bonestell and George Pal
full marks for these. The takeoff is from a long ramp which, for some
unexplained reason, dips down into a valley and then goes up the

From the Journal of the British Interplanetary Society *11, no. 1
(1952): 1–3. Reprinted by permission.*

side of a mountain. (The only effect of such a dip, of course, would be to waste a certain amount of gravitational energy.) The ship itself is winged, so that it can make an atmospheric landing on the new planet—which for some reason has had its name changed from the book's sensible "Bronson Beta" to "Zyra."

Some of the scenes of destruction on the first approach of the invaders are superbly done—genuine disasters being skilfully combined with model work to produce a really terrifying sequence. The takeoff is also very well contrived, and one of the moments which lives in the memory is the last view of the launching site, bathed in a ghastly yellow light from the star which now fills the sky.

By keeping the travelers in this interplanetary Noah's Ark strapped in their seats, the producer neatly avoids grappling with the problem of weightlessness. ("Zyra" is apparently so close that the whole voyage only lasts an hours or so.) The landing among the mountains of the new world, on a convenient snow field, is dramatic enough, but what should be the big moment of the film is completely ruined. When the door of the spaceship is flung open (as someone rightly says: "Why test the air? We've nowhere else to go!") the snow has mysteriously vanished and we are confronted with a crude back cloth which is more like off-colour Disney than vintage Bonestell.

Since the film does not attempt technical accuracy on the scale of *Destination Moon*, it is unfair to make detailed criticism of it on this score. One would, however, have imagined that it was obvious even to the most unscientific that the first spaceship could hardly be built from scratch in a fraction of the time necessary to design and construct a perfectly conventional airplane—especially when civilization was collapsing on all sides. One also wonders what the average picturegoer will think of astronomical accuracy when he sees one group of astronomers, equipped with differential analysers and all modern conveniences, producing a prediction which is flatly denied by another group who presumably have the same facilities. (To anyone who remarks that astronomers are *always* disagreeing, and points to Fred Hoyle in proof, we would testily reply that there is not much room for argument over a simple problem in celestial mechanics.)

On balance, *When Worlds Collide* certainly contains enough interesting material to make it worth a visit. Whether any producer of lesser genius than D. W. Griffith could have handled this theme properly is a subject on which everyone will have their own opinion.

Don't Play with Fire
by PIERRE KAST

As a literary genre, science fiction looks to the future in the same way as the historical novel looks to the past. "Historical novel" applies to *The Clansman* as well as *War and Peace*, to *Forever Amber* as well as *I, Claudius*. Thus the rather severe critics who have condemned science fiction on the evidence of its space operas have been a little too hasty. . . . Science fiction is a harmonious synthesis of fantasy in the style of Poe, Swiftian satire, and anticipation à la Jules Verne. In it, the best complaisantly rubs shoulders with the worst; the best, however, is an extraordinary stimulant of the epic imagination, and it can now be said that Ray Bradbury, Murray Leinster, and A. E. Van Vogt are writers of the very first rank.

In addition to giving free rein to one's wildest dreams, science fiction makes another important contribution to literature: it revolutionizes the relationship between man and the universe. Man is no longer the heart of the universe; he is no longer extending his powers over it as in Verne or Wells. Relativism has thrust its way into popular literature, so that Earth has become no more than a pebble in space, while man may be no more than a dull brute in the eyes of galactic civilizations. (As a matter of fact, our generals, policemen, and colonial puppets have already given us this idea, without having anything to do with popular literature.) Though science fiction at its best is uncompromisingly relativistic and pessimistic, it has acquired a large following in the United States and the Soviet Union, and is at least known in France. The cinema was bound to take notice of it.

Needless to say, the masterminds of film production have shown

From Cahiers du Cinéma, *no. 12 (May 1952): 70–71. Copyright ©
1952 by Les Éditions de l'Étoile. Reprinted by permission of Les
Éditions de l'Étoile and Grove Press, Inc.*

most interest in space opera. Thus we have seen a stupid, dull, and puerile film of realism, *Destination Moon,* and a stupid, dull, and puerile horror film, *The Thing.* To hold science fiction responsible for these films would be like blaming Stendhal for the idiocies of Christian-Jaque. It goes without saying that the childish socio-economic structure of film production gives rise to childish films. *The Day the Earth Stood Still,* a film by Robert Wise, has nothing in common with such nonsense.

One recalls the inner violence, the repressed rage, the shuddering impassivity of *The Setup.* Wise's new film shows no slackening, no concessions. Since *Monsieur Verdoux,* I have seen no other American film so improbably made in America. The film is a long, secret cry of agony, the expression of a terrible vertigo. It is almost literally stunning.

An alien arrives from another world which is more mature and civilized than our divided, ravaged, and childishly destructive Earth. He has come to give mankind a solemn warning: "Don't play with the atomic bomb. You are irresponsible children whose powers exceed your wisdom. Grow up, or stop playing with fire." The man from space loses himself in American society, passing through a world of boarding houses, radio news flashes, the FBI, witch hunts, the Pentagon, and cops. The violence of the satire is sharply reinforced by a total moral relativism. "Taking a detached view" is an expression which, until now, has been used by reactionaries to let cops beat up strikers. Robert Wise and Harry Bates use it to ridicule the divine right of Western civilization. I have a suspicious horror of messages, but it was disarmed by the brilliance of the film's action and its cinematic form.

Like *The Setup, The Day the Earth Stood Still* is a film about evil and violence. The dispute between montage and deep focus is no longer relevant. Robert Wise shows that there are not two schools of filmmaking but only one—the school of effectiveness. He plays no favorites between camera movement and cutting: at one moment it is a quick cut, the next moment a long and complex scene which packs the punch. All that's required is that the technique used should fit the situation. A statement of the obvious? It might be, in a realm of cinematic absolutes where each end would have its own means. One virtue of Wise's film—and not the least one, either —is that it whispers in our ear the timely reminder that there are no absolutes. "You know," the U.S. President's secretary tells the alien, "there are on Earth the forces of good and the forces of evil.

We are the forces of good." "I'm not interested in such foolishness,"
says the alien. Clearly, this is a far cry from corn-fed physicists looking for the American way of life on the moon, one finger on the
trigger of their secret weapons.

Of course, this is only a film. But it takes a lot of impudence and
daring on Robert Wise's part to skim over the taboos of his country's Establishment. His film goes far enough in revealing the profound alienation of man in our ridiculous civilization, and in mocking the so-called values of our moral and political system, for it to
gain our sympathy, even though the visitor it brings from Arcturus
or wherever still looks like a handsome film star. The bloodthirsty
thinking carrot in *The Thing* gave the military the chance to score
a smashing victory. But when Klaatu leaves Earth, no one in the
audience feels like making a joke, no one feels triumphant or
vindicated. The film ends on a poignant, questioning note, stressing
the fatal limitations of man; yet strangely enough, these limitations
apply not to the weak nature of man as an individual but to man
as a social animal, accepting a certain way of life. Robert Wise is
not fired by the holy misanthropy of Pascal, but comes closer to the
fury of Swift. He does not condemn the thinking reeds themselves,
but their form of society.

In countless ways the film makes one aware of the intelligence
and tough-mindedness behind it. In countless ways it reveals originality, boldness, and irreverence. I cannot help liking it very much
indeed.

INVASION OF THE BODY SNATCHERS
by ERNESTO G. LAURA

One day, in an American small town named Santa Mira, some people suddenly become aware that their fathers or sisters or sons are no longer "themselves." There is no change in their appearance, behavior, or character, but they seem somehow to have been emptied inside, as if they had "no emotion—none—only the pretense of it." Next day, all the people who had this impression about someone in their family are laughing at it, saying they must have suffered from some odd kind of hallucination.

That is the starting point of *Invasion of the Body Snatchers*, a science fiction film that is only now appearing on Italian screens, about a year after its American release. The film is of interest both for the seriousness with which is was made—something unusual in a genre which, while growing in popularity, normally has to be content with second-rate directors and scriptwriters—and for the theme behind its fantastic story. In fact, the allegorical meaning becomes clearer and clearer as the action unfolds. Mysterious pods arrive from some unknown source, and each of them transforms itself into a body identical to that of the nearest human being. It then replaces that person, absorbing his personality without his humanity—since the pods are and remain vegetables. They are also a symbol whose message is easy to read.

Considering the state of public opinion in the United States today, from the recent wave of McCarthyism to the fear of a third World War, it is natural to see the pods as standing for the idea of communism which gradually takes possession of a normal person, leaving him outwardly unchanged but transformed within. This is the kind of simple-minded presentation of the problem that can be found in *Reader's Digest*, but it corresponds to the average Ameri-

From Bianco e Nero *18, no. 12 (1957): 69–71. Reprinted by permission.*

can's views as they have been shaped by television and a wide range of periodicals. The memory of Orwell and his *1984* is still very much alive. Anglo-Saxon literature in general shows a predilection for allegory, and so does its more recent popular subdivision, science fiction: H. G. Wells, widely regarded as the founder of modern science fiction, was a typically allegorical writer. The fact that allegory is the key to *Invasion of the Body Snatchers* readily becomes apparent when one looks at the book on which it is based, Jack Finney's *The Body Snatchers*. In this unpretentious popular novel, the arrival of the pods is accounted for as an invasion from outer space, and there are quite detailed pseudoscientific explanations of how the "twinning" is accomplished, how long it takes, and so on.

Don Siegel has dropped all this, leaving the mystery unexplained. One morning we wake up and find a huge pod in the cellar; it splits open, revealing a blank which develops and takes on the shape of our body; and it waits for the time when our consciousness is at its weakest, when we are asleep at night, to take possession of us. With its atmosphere of unexplained mystery, the action of the film acquires a remarkable power of suggestion which reveals that Siegel, until now a competent craftsman, has a personality of his own. His background, which includes schooling at Cambridge University in England and serious training for the theater, has undoubtedly influenced the careful dramatic structure of the film, full of suspense but at the same time controlled, free of excesses.

In the film as in the novel, Miles, the protagonist, remains the only inhabitant of Santa Mira to hold out, fighting against sleep to preserve his freedom. Then, in the novel, Miles sets fire to the field where the pods are being grown: those that are not destroyed by the flames rise up into the sky, quitting the planet which has shown itself so hostile to them. "We hadn't, and couldn't possibly have been . . . the only souls who had stumbled and blundered onto what had been happening in Santa Mira. There'd been others, of course, individuals, and little groups . . . who had fought, struggled, and simply refused to give up. Some others may have won, many had lost, but all of us who had not been caught and trapped without a chance had fought implacably, and a fragment of a wartime speech moved through my mind: 'We shall fight them in the fields, and in the streets, we shall fight in the hills; we shall never surrender.'" Clearly, having had little success with his allegory, the author of the book falls back on preaching, spelling out the facile McCarthyism of his message.

With better dramatic sense, Siegel ends with Miles running onto a highway. While truck after truck sets out from Santa Mira loaded with pods for the rest of the world, Miles yells the danger to automobile drivers who take no notice as they roar past him. It is a powerful and convincing sequence. While the film is no masterpiece, it is stimulating for its sidelights on the views and attitudes of average Americans, and it is noteworthy for the hallucinatory atmosphere conferred on it by a hitherto minor director.

Interview with Don Siegel
by GUY BRAUCOURT

. . . Invasion of the Body Snatchers, *which wasn't discovered in France until a dozen years after it was made, is one of the greatest science fiction films.*

It is in fact my favorite film, which doesn't mean that it's my best work but that it's the most interesting subject I've ever filmed. I had a lot of difficulties at the time because the studio was against the film, while Producer Walter Wanger, scriptwriter Daniel Mainwaring, the actors, and I all firmly believed in it, as we saw how well the shooting was going. I remember a joke I played on the leading lady, Dana Wynter, while we were shooting. We were all living in separate bungalows, and Dana's was more isolated than the rest. One day I went and tapped at her window, and when she came out to see what was happening I slipped into her bedroom with one of the pods used in the film and left it there. A moment later we saw her come running out, white-faced and speechless—that's how much she believed in the film!

What happened in the States at that time was that if a film didn't have a big budget or impressive credits with top stars, the critics ignored it. Since then things have changed a little, but not much. Anyway, no one took any notice of the film when it was first released, especially as the studio had inflicted a ridiculous title on it, over my objections. I wanted to call it simply *Sleep No More.* But little by little movie lovers and student groups began to take an interest in the film and give it a reputation, so that it has ended up being very well known.

I believe the studio added the prologue and epilogue, which put

From Image et Son, *April 1970, pp. 80–84. Reprinted by permission of the Ligue Française d'Enseignement Permanente and the author.*

the main action in a frame and opened up the possibility of a happy ending.

There were three previews of the film the way I'd made it, and the audiences reacted in an extraordinary way, just as I'd hoped. They started out by laughing, but then the tension increased and they ended up thoroughly scared. The final scene was the one where the hero runs out into the highway, trying to stop a car, and he points his finger at one of the drivers—in reality, at the audience—shouting "You're next!" like in a trial. But having heard the audiences laugh, the studio thought that the public was reacting against the film, and didn't realize what the laughter really meant. I was opposed to making any changes, but Walter Wanger, who was on my side, persuaded me that it was better to do them myself, in the same style and spirit as the rest of the film, because someone was going to make the changes anyway and they might very well compromise what we'd already planned and shot. So I decided to add the prologue and epilogue. But let me repeat that all of us who worked on the film believed in what it said—that the majority of people in the world unfortunately are pods, existing without any intellectual aspirations and incapable of love.

Some critics have seen the film as a parable about the spread of fascism. Is that too farfetched an interpretation?

At the outset, neither the scriptwriter nor I had that in mind. What we wanted to attack was much more a general state of mind that is found in everyday life. As the director I found it much more exciting, instead of seeing the story as a fascist plot, to show how a very ordinary state of mind could start out in a very quiet small town and spread to a whole country. But it's certainly possible to make the interpretation you mention, I've no objection to it at all. In any case, I think it arises quite naturally because the aim of fascism is that people under its rule should be like that, having no emotions or personality, like vegetables.

Why have you never made any other science fiction films?

First of all, because the special-effects side of them frightens me off a bit. I worked on special effects for seven years, and I did an enormous amount of second unit work on action sequences, and when I started out as a director there were attempts to lock me into action and special-effects films. I refused to be typecast that way, and when I found myself with a science fiction subject, I decided right from the start to take the opposite approach to what's usually done in the genre—lots of trick shots, sets, and machinery, and, stuck in front of them, some wooden actors whose faces show no expression except a bit of terror now and then! So I said to the producer, "Don't worry, there's no need to set aside 90 per cent of the budget for special effects, we're going to give priority to the action and characters." . . . It's not that I'm categorically opposed to special effects, it's just that I'm not interested in seeing them get more attention than the story. . . .

TAKING STOCK: SOME ISSUES AND ANSWERS

A Brief, Tragical History
of the Science Fiction Film
by RICHARD HODGENS

> *Cut is the branch that might have grown
> full straight,
> And burned is Apollo's laurel-bough,
> That sometime grew within this
> learned man.
> Faustus is gone: regard his hellish fall,
> Whose fiendful fortune may exhort the
> wise,
> Only to wonder at unlawful things,
> Whose deepness doth entice such
> forward wits
> To practise more than heavenly power
> permits.*
>
> —*Doctor Faustus,* Epilogue

Some of the most original and thoughtful contemporary fiction has been science fiction, and this field may well prove to be of much greater literary importance than is generally admitted. In motion pictures, however, "science fiction" has so far been unoriginal and limited; and both the tone and the implications of these films suggest a strange throwback of taste to something moldier and more "Gothic" than the Gothic novel. But the genre is an interesting and potentially very fruitful one.

Science fiction publishing expanded spectacularly in the late '40s, and dwindled again in the early '50s. Science fiction filming as we know it today began in 1950 with *Destination Moon,* and has continued to the present, hideously transformed, as a minor category

From Film Quarterly *13, no. 2 (1959): 30–39. Copyright © 1959 by the Regents of the University of California. Reprinted by permission of the Regents and the author.*

of production. Earlier examples, like Fritz Lang's *Metropolis* and *Frau im Mond,* H. G. Wells's powerful essay on future history, *Things to Come,* and such nonsupernatural horror films as *The Invisible Ray,* have not been considered "science fiction," although they were. One of the many painful aspects of most of the recent films involving space travel, alien visitors, or earthly monsters which have followed *Destination Moon* is that they *are* considered "science fiction," although most of them are something peculiarly different from the literature of the same label.

Motion-picture adaptations have ruined any number of good works of literature without casting a pall, in the public mind, over literature in general. The science fiction films, however, seem to have come close to ruining the reputation of the category of fiction from which they have malignantly sprouted. To the film audience, "science fiction" means "horror," distinguished from ordinary horror only by a relative lack of plausibility.

Science fiction involves extrapolated or fictitious science, or fictitious use of scientific possibilities, or it may be simply fiction that takes place in the future or introduces some radical assumption about the present or the past. For those who insist upon nothing but direct treatment of contemporary life, science fiction has little or nothing to offer, of course. But there are issues that cannot be dealt with realistically in terms of the present, or even the past; and to confront such issues in fiction it is better to invent a future-tense society than to distort the present or the past. And in a broader sense there are few subjects that cannot be considered in science fiction, few styles in which it cannot be written, and few moods that it cannot convey. It is, to my mind, the only kind of writing today that offers much surprise—not merely the surprise of shock effects, but the surprise of new or unusual material handled rationally. And conscientious science fiction, more than any other type, offers the reader that shift of focus essential to the appeal of any literature. Often too it presents a puzzle analogous to that of the detective story, but with its central assumptions considerably less restricted.

Science fiction, as most science fiction readers define it and as most science fiction writers attempt to practice it, calls for a plausible or at least possible premise, logically developed. The most damning criticism one can make of a work of science fiction is that it is flatly impossible in the first place, and inconsistent in the second. To say the least, many things are possible; and readers may accept a premise that they believe impossible anyway, so long as they do not consider it "supernatural." Often, the distinction between science fiction and fantasy is simply one of attitude; but an impossible premise must at least not contradict itself, and it should be developed consistently in the story.

Science fiction films, with few exceptions, follow different conventions. The premise is always flatly impossible. Any explanations offered are either false analogy or entirely meaningless. The character who protests "But that's *incredible, Doctor!"* is always right. The impossible, and often self-contradictory, premise is irrationally developed, if it is developed at all. There is less narrative logic than in the average Western.

Although antiscientific printed science fiction exists, most science fiction reflects at least an awareness and appreciation of science. Some science fiction, it is true, displays an uncomprehending faith in science, and implies that it will solve all problems magically. But in the SF films there is rarely any sane middle ground. Now and then, science is white magic. But far more often, it is black, and if these films have any general implications about science, they are that science and scientists are dangerous, raising problems and provoking widespread disaster for the innocent, ignorant good folks, and that curiosity is a deadly sin. The few exceptions to this bleak picture are the first three SF films produced by George Pal: *Destination Moon, When Worlds Collide,* and *War of the Worlds.* Perhaps there are one or two others. *Destination Moon* may be considered a good semidocumentary, educational film, although today its optimism is rather depressing. Despite its accuracy and consistency, and the extent to which the stereotyped characters were forced to go to explain it, most criticism indicated that the critics did not understand it. The special effects were the film's main attraction, and except for a few shots of the apparent size of the ship in space, and the appearance of the stars, were exact and superb. . . .

Those who hoped that the financial success of *Destination Moon* would lead to equally convincing but more sophisticated science fiction films were bitterly disappointed, for nearly everything since has been unconvincing and naive. There was a flood of "science fiction" on the screen, but it followed in the footsteps of *The Thing,* and it was unbelievably and progressively inane.

Pal's next two productions were satisfactory, however, and although they are not very impressive when compared with a film like *Things to Come,* in comparison with their contemporary science fiction competition they seemed masterpieces. In the '30s Paramount had considered *When Worlds Collide*, a novel by Edwin Balmer and Philip Wylie, for De Mille, and *War of the Worlds*, by H. G. Wells, for Eisenstein. Pal's films modernized the sources, but respected them. Unlike *Destination Moon*, however, both have themes of menace and catastrophe—the end of the world and interplanetary invasion. It appeared that even Pal had decided that SF films must be, somehow, *horrible.*

In *When Worlds Collide*, models were used extensively, and while many of them were not completely convincing, the only major disappointment to most people was the last shot of the lush, green new world, after the single escaping spaceship had landed in impressively rugged territory. H. G. Wells's *War of the Worlds* is a good novel, and difficult to ruin. If *War of the Worlds* had been filmed as a period piece as Disney later treated Jules Verne's *20,000 Leagues Under the Sea*, it would still have been effective. The story was carefully modernized, however, as Howard Koch had modernized it in 1938 for Orson Welles's Mercury Theater of the Air. One unnecessary modern addition, though, was an irrelevant boy-and-girl theme because, Pal apologized, "Audiences want it." [1]

The theme of Wells's memorable "assault on human self-satisfaction" is still valid, if less startling. No one today expects to be visited by intelligent Martians, but granting this premise the film was quite convincing. The Martians' fantastic weapons were acceptable as products of a superior technology; the Martians themselves, though more terrestrial in appearance than Wells's original conception, were probably the most convincing Things to come from Hollywood, and they were used with surprising restraint and effectiveness—one brief glimpse and, at the end, a lingering shot of the hand of the dying creature. About half the film was painstaking special effect, and the models were nearly perfect.

These three films were spectacular productions, and if the scripts contained moments rather similar to more traditional spectacles, they still contained powerful images that had never been seen before: after takeoff, virtually every shot in *Destination Moon;* the red dwarf star nearing the doomed Earth; and the deadly Martian machines, like copper mantas and hooded cobras, gliding down empty streets.

I do not mean to imply that everyone was pleased by these films. Those who like plots with villains were bored by *Destination Moon,*

---

[1] "Filming War of the Worlds," *Astounding Science Fiction,* October 1953.

and people who knew nothing about space travel, and did not care, were baffled. *When Worlds Collide* drew harsh words for its concluding shot and its models, and some people seem to have been irritated by the undemocratic survival of the interplanetary Ark. And of *War of the Worlds* I heard someone say, "That Orson Welles always was crazy, anyway."

George Pal's last science fiction production, *The Conquest of Space,* was disappointing. Again there were some visually impressive shots, but unfortunately that was all. The script attempted to "enliven" a subject that called for serious treatment; the result was an inaccurate, misleading film ending with a miracle which, unlike the "miraculous" end of *War,* was impossible and pointless. It was an expensive production which could have contributed to the salvation of science fiction in motion pictures. But the monsters had taken the field, and the facile *Conquest of Space* merely seemed to prove that monsters are always necessary.

What the movies were likely to do with science fiction was already evident when *Rocketship X-M* was released in 1950 to compete with *Destination Moon.* An expedition sets out for the moon. The ship's course is altered by the close passage of some noisy meteors, however, and the explorers land on Mars, where they learn that atomic warfare has destroyed Martian civilization. The Martians appear to be entirely human—at least, if memory serves, one savage female was beautifully human—but radiation has bestialized them. The girl scientist and the boy scientist escape from Mars, but, lacking fuel to land on the frantically spinning Earth, they endure a stoic martyrdom. Though *Rocketship X-M* seemed ludicrous, it was level-headed and superb compared with what followed.

The great villain was *The Thing from Another World,* which appeared in 1951. *The Thing* was based on a short novel by John W. Campbell, Jr., the editor of *Astounding Science Fiction,* where it appeared in 1938 with the title "Who Goes There?" The story is regarded as one of the most original and effective science fiction stories, *subspecies* "horror." Its premise is convincing, its development logical, its characterization intelligent, and its suspense considerable. Of these qualities the film retained one or two minutes of suspense. The story and the film are poles apart. Probably for timely interest, the Thing crashed in a flying saucer and was quick-frozen in the Arctic. In Campbell's story "it had lain in the ice for twenty million years" in the Antarctic. In film as in source, when the creature thaws out it is alive and dangerous. In "Who Goes There?,"

when it gets up and walks away, and later when it is torn to pieces
by the dogs and still lives, the nature of the beast makes its invulner-
ability acceptable. But there is little plausibility about the Hollywood Thing's nine lives. Since this film, presumably dead creatures
have been coming back to life with more and more alacrity and
with less and less excuse. Instead of the nearly insoluble problem
created in Campbell's story, this Thing is another monster entirely.
He is a vegetable. He looks like Frankenstein's monster. He roars.
He is radioactive. And he drinks blood.[2]

Probably Campbell's protean menace was reduced to this strange
combination of familiar elements in the belief that the original idea
—the idea which made the story make sense—was too complex. This
was probably incorrect, because monsters since that *Thing* have imi-
tated the special ability of Campbell's Alien, although with far less
credibility (*It Came from Outer Space, Invasion of the Body
Snatchers*), and there is no indication that anyone found them difficult to understand.

Incidentally, the most stupid character in the film is the most
important scientist. The script did its best to imply that his tolerant
attitude toward the Thing was his worst idea. And the film ended
with a warning to all mankind: "Watch the skies" for these abomina-
bly dangerous Flying Saucers.

The Thing is a most radical betrayal of its source, but since the
source was generally unfamiliar, and since the idea of a monster
from outer space seemed so original (though the monster itself had
blood brothers in Transylvania), the film earned both critical approval and a great deal of money.[3] In addition, it fixed the pattern
for the majority of science fiction films that followed, for it proved
that some money could be made by "science fiction" that preyed on
current fears symbolized crudely by any preposterous monster, and
the only special expense involved would be for one monster suit.

Not all SF films since *The Thing* have been about monsters, but
the majority have. *The Day the Earth Stood Still*, also released in
1951, was almost, but not quite, a monster film. It was not a story
of catastrophe as the title suggests, but of alien visitors. The screen-

---

[2] It may be pointed out that Wells's Martians shared this improbable habit;
but they were not vegetable bipeds, and that was about fifty years before.

[3] Vague approval of this film is found even today, when its "novelty" is no
excuse. For instance, Frank Hauser, although aware of the fiction of Bradbury
and Heinlein, makes this wild understatement: "The film, unfortunately, was
not entirely successful." (In his "Science Fiction Films," in William Whitebait's
International Film Annual, No. 2, New York: Doubleday, 1958).

play deprived another popular science fiction story from *Astounding*, Harry Bates's "Farewell to the Master," of its good ideas, its conviction, and its point. *The Day* substituted a message: Earthlings, behave yourselves. Again, probably because like *The Thing* the story was novel but could be understood without much effort, *The Day* earned good reviews and good money. Whatever reservations one may have about the film, in comparison with *The Thing* and its spawn, *The Day* has a comparatively civilized air, at least.

It Came from Outer Space was another rare exception that appeared rather early in the Cycle. One of the virtues of *It Came from Outer Space* is that It is here by accident, and wants to go home.

Following the precedent that *The Thing* set, *The Beast from 20,000 Fathoms* and *Them!* established major variations of the monster theme. *The Beast* was an amphibious dinosaur. I cannot remember whether nuclear physics was responsible for its resuscitation or its final destruction, but probably it was both. *The Beast*, like *The Thing*, thaws to life, but it was a menace of terrestrial origin. This simplifies the filmmakers' problems. *The Beast* has been followed by several monsters revived, we are told, from the distant past, and all of them instinctively attack populous cities. (*King Kong*, unlike these "atom beasts," had some sort of motivation.) *Them!* were giant ants, also dangerous, in the sewers of Los Angeles. Impossibly large insects with a taste for human flesh had appeared in *The Deadly Mantis*, *The Spider*, and others. The milder *Creature from the Black Lagoon* proved so popular that he himself returned for *Revenge*, but of all the earthly monsters, only *The Magnetic Monster*, with a script by Curt Siodmak, displayed much originality and consistency.

The Incredible Shrinking Man created its bloated-insect horror by shrinking the hero until an ordinary spider became typically perilous. The unfortunate young man of the title passes through a strange cloud while sunbathing on his cabin cruiser and begins to shrink—evenly, all over. The screenplay, by Richard Matheson from his own novel, is a protracted and occasionally amusing agony. Soon the incredible shrinking man is too small to live an ordinary life. He finds brief happiness with a beautiful midget, but he breaks off their relationship when he discovers that he has become too short for her. He is plagued by reporters. When his wife walks downstairs, the doll house in which he lives shakes with unbearable violence. The cat chases him. He gets lost in the cellar. Then the spider chases him. Although the premise of the story is impossible, the end improves upon it, for the incredible shrinking man does not die because "in the mind of God there is no zero." Even God, in the science fiction films, is a poor mathematician. *The Shrinking Man* began its own minor series of increasingly poor films about people who are too small or too big. . . .

Invasions from space did not cease. *The Blob* came in color, and Martian Blood Rust sprouted in black and white in *Spacemaster X-7*. When Japan is invaded by *The Mysterians* the aggressors' one insupportable demand is intermarriage with human females "because there is so much strontium-90 in our bones." If one can safely judge by title and advertising, *I Married a Monster from Outer Space* involves a similar unlikely prospect, and takes the same attitude toward it. This is like expecting the Thing to pollinate Godzilla, but monstrous union is in line with this sort of film, and, considering the attitude they display toward almost every Thing in them, an intolerant view of mixed marriage is to be expected. The Mysterians, incidentally, look very much like human beings, except that they melt. Space travel is rare in SF films now, but we have discovered human beings native to Mars, Venus, and various nonexistent planets. Sometimes space travel and monsters are ingeniously combined, as when *The First Man into Space* returns a monster. *The Forbidden Planet* and *This Island Earth* were expensive color productions which involved space travel and managed to have their monsters too. In *Forbidden Planet* it had something to do with the id, but it might as well have been Grendel. *This Island Earth,* an unbelievable adaptation of a somewhat less unbelievable novel by Raymond F. Jones, included a horrendous Thing called, of all things, a "Mutant."

The most recent big SF film is *The Fly,* in CinemaScope and Horror-color, and popular enough to call for a Return. . . . *The Fly* is not from the short story of that title by Arthur Porges, originally in *The Magazine of Fantasy and Science Fiction,* but from another story of the same title by George Langelaan, originally in *Playboy*. Porges' story presents an interesting situation which could not be filmed without expansion and, inevitably, ruination; and it would be called *Invasion of the Atom-Fly from Another World*. Since Langelaan's story is impossible to begin with, is inconsistent anyway, and is a horror story as horrifying as the most horrible SF films, one might expect that it could endure motion-picture adaptation. The film, however, managed to be more impossible and less consistent, to add clichés and bright blood, and to contrive a happier ending with some morally repugnant implications.

Even if one accepts, for the sake of entertainment, the initial premise that André Delambre has built, in his basement, a working matter-transmitter, nothing else follows. The machine behaves differently each time it makes a mistake. The molecular structure of a dish is reversed. A cat, with a pitiable wail, disappears entirely. Finally, André himself is somehow mixed up with a fly. The result is a handsome scientist with ". . . the head of a fly" (and an arm, too) and "the fly with the head of a man!" [4] Of course, there is a certain ingenuity about the accident: it creates two "monsters" instead of one. But why is André with the head of the fly still André, and why does his fly-leg have (evidently) a fly's volition? Why was the part of the fly grafted to André enlarged to fit him so well? How does he eat? Breathe? Why does he gradually begin to think a bit like a fly, and why is he then tempted to maul his poor wife, Helene? Why destroy the lab? The series of physical impossibilities in the script is not helped by the psychology. After squashing the man with the head of the fly in a hydraulic press, Helene neither commits suicide nor is confined, as in the story. Helene is saved from grief and inconvenience by Commissaire Charas who, at the last minute, notes the fly with the head of a man, and squashes it with a rock. What else, indeed, could be done with it? Although it is clear that André's death (*i.e.*, André$_1$, in the press) was suicide in which Helene cooperated, the script chooses to ignore the moral problem presented by the suicide, or the mercy killing, or whatever it was. Instead, the issue is that Helene killed a mere Thing. After all, it is not improper to kill a Thing, and one may safely kill a man if he is no longer entirely human. This follows repetitious dialogue about the Sacredness of Life, but apparently they meant natural, original life-forms only, and the cat is more sacred than André in either combination. In the last scene of the film, André's surviving brother delivers a little pro-science speech to André's son while Helene listens, smiling sweetly. Father, the boy's uncle tells him, was like Columbus. What will be remembered, of course, is that Father was like a fly.

The Fly, like most SF films, has a rather strange, very old moral.

---

[4] In the story, André attempts to rectify this error and merely mixes himself with the vanished cat as well as the housefly; this explains why the author did away with the cat, if not how. No doubt the makers of the film considered this too complicated, but retained the cat's disappearance for the unique poignancy of the scene.

1. Melies's *A Trip to the Moon*. Photo courtesy The Museum of Modern Art/Film Stills Archive.

2. *2001: A Space Odyssey.* Copyright © 1968 by Metro-Goldwyn-Mayer, Inc. Reprinted by permission of Metro-Goldwyn-Mayer, Inc.

3. *Woman in the Moon.* Photo courtesy The Museum of Modern Art/Film Stills Archive.

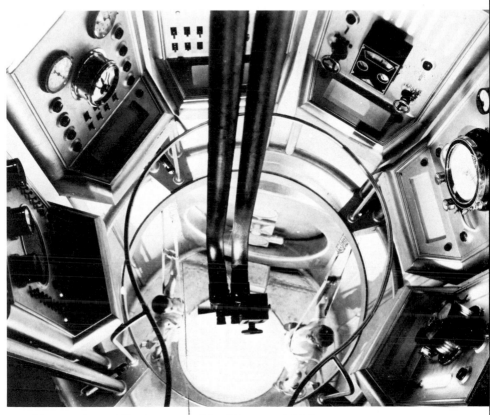

4. *Things to Come.* Photo courtesy The Museum of Modern Art/Film Stills Archive.

5. *Destination Moon*. Copyright 1950, An Eagle Lion Film. Reprinted by permission of Norman Freeman.

6. *Destination Moon*. Copyright 1950, An Eagle Lion Film. Reprinted by permission of Norman Freeman.

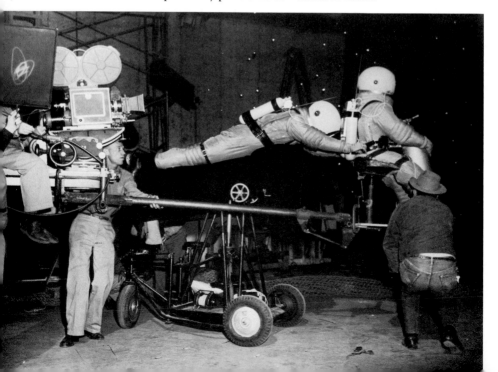

7. *War of the Worlds.* Copyright 1952 by Paramount Pictures Corporation. Reprinted by permission of Paramount Pictures Corporation.

8. *Invasion of the Body Snatchers.* Reprinted by permission of Allied Artists.

9. *Forbidden Planet.* Copyright © 1956 by Metro-Goldwyn-Mayer, Inc. Photo courtesy The Museum of Modern Art/Film Stills Archive. Reprinted by permission of Metro-Goldwyn-Mayer, Inc.

10. *Ikarie XB1 (Voyage to the End of the Universe).* © American International Television, Inc., 1969. Reprinted by permission of American International Television, Inc.

11. *These Are the Damned*. Reprinted by permission of Hammer
Film Productions.

12. *Fahrenheit 451.* Copyright 1966 Universal Pictures. Reprinted by permission of Universal Pictures.

A search for knowledge or any worldly improvements may go too far; it may be blasphemous; and one may be punished with an unnatural end.[5]

The premises of SF films are all antique, and carelessly handled. Twenty years ago, the matter-transmitter in the present-day cellar might have been almost convincing; but now one would expect it in a more credible context, and expect it to function with some consistency. Most SF films, however, do not take place in the future, where such an invention might be acceptable. *1984* is a rare, recent exception; but if Orwell's novel had not forced the date, it would have been 1960.

It is true that magazine science fiction developed and exploited the stereotyped mad scientist and the evil bug-eyed monster. But that, again, was about twenty years ago. Giant insects, shrinking men, and dinosaurs can be found in science fiction of the same period. It is true that some science fiction stories are as unoriginal, illogical, and monstrous as SF films; but you have to know where to look in order to find many of them.

Apart from such incidental lessons as the immorality of attempting to prolong life and the advisability of forgetting anything new that one happens to learn, there are two vague ideas that appear in SF films with some regularity. Sometimes, the menace or the Thing does not merely kill its victims, but deprives them of their identity, their free will, or their individual rights and obligations as members of a free society. In *Attack of the Puppet People,* for instance, the combination dollmaker and mad superscientist who shrinks the people he likes is a sort of pathetic, benevolent dictator. Many SF films derive whatever emotional effect they have from their half-hearted allegorization of the conflict between individuality and conformity. Usually, the conflict remains undeveloped, and although the characters tend to resist such menaces, their reasons may often be that the menace is a slimy, repulsive Thing, or that they would resist any change, even one for the better. *1984* is the only SF film that took this conflict as its subject, although it is common in science fiction novels.

The other vague idea is that atomic power is dangerous. The point has been made again and again, ever since the Geiger counter reacted to the presence of the first Thing. The point is indisputable,

[5] In *The Return of the Fly,* the same thing happens, and the moral is the same.

but these films rarely show any awareness of the ways in which the atom is dangerous. The danger of atomic war is explicit in Arch Oboler's *Five,* the recent *The World, the Flesh, and the Devil,* and the forthcoming *On the Beach.* These films are not only exceptional, they are not generally considered to be science fiction. In the ordinary science fiction film, atomic bombs raise dragons and shrink people. Even *The Fly,* which had nothing to do with the effects of radiation, real or imagined, was advertised as if its poor monsters were the realistic, possible outcome of fallout on flesh. It may be argued that all the atomic monsters of SF films are symbols, and I suppose that they are, but they are inapt, inept, or both.

If the creators of monster films had intended any comment on the problems raised by the atomic bomb, or even on feelings about it, as some kindly critics have assumed, they would not have made their monster films at all. The most obvious advantage of science fiction, and the three films mentioned above, is that one can deal with such problems and feelings by extending the situation into the future and showing a possible effect or resolution. There is no need for indirect discussion or for a plot with a "symbol" as its mainspring. A twelve-ton, woman-eating cockroach does not say anything about the bomb simply because it, too, is radioactive, or crawls out of a test site, and the filmmakers have simply attempted to make their monster more frightening by associating it with something serious.

One should realize that, like them or not, the invaders in Wells's *War of the Worlds,* the stranded Alien in Campbell's "Who Goes There?," or the parasites in Heinlein's *Puppet Masters* (clumsily parodied by *The Brain Eaters,* who are complex parasitic animals that evolved when there were no hosts for them) are a different sort of monster from those of most SF films. They may be symbols too, but first they are beings. Campbell may invent a creature that evokes a complex of ancient fears—fear of the ancient itself, the fear that death may not be final, that evil is indestructible, and fear rising from the imitation motif, fear of possession, of loss of identity, all the fears that gave rise to tales of demons, ghosts, witches, vampires, shape-shifters. But in "Who Goes There?" it is a realistically conceived being that evokes these fears and creates the suspense, not an impossible symbol; and the story is not hysterical, but a study of man under stress.

The SF films abuse their borrowed props and offer nothing but hysteria. The films resemble unpleasant dreams, but rarely resemble them well. One cannot condemn an attempt to make a film suggesting nightmare illogic, of course. But surrealism is not what the makers of these films have in mind.

Fantasy and science fiction are not convincing if they are not consistent. Convincing the audience to accept the initial premise of the story may be difficult enough, without violating that premise in each scene. Expensive and careful treatment of a careless script cannot overcome the script's bad logic in science fiction or anything else. And while careful SF scripts are rare, careful treatment is even more rare. Most of the special effects in SF films, for instance, would not deceive a myopic child in the back of the theater—not even all the third-degree burns and running sores that have become so popular. The films convey the impression that everyone involved is aware that he is working on something which is not only beneath his talent but beneath the audience as well. It seems that even the makeup department, called upon by the pointless turns of a morbid plot to disintegrate a bored actor, has neither the time nor the heart to waste any effort, and produces something that looks like the unraveling of an old vacuum-cleaner bag. Perhaps this is a good thing. But it is strange that if you hire a group of talented people and ask for another science fiction horror, you will get a film that is not merely abominable in conception and perverse in implication but half-hearted in execution.

Reginald Bretnor's symposium, *Modern Science Fiction* (New York: Coward-McCann), contains an interesting article by Don Fabun, "Science Fiction in Motion Pictures, Radio, and Television," a detailed examination that concludes with this hope: "In time we may see the modern literary form called science fiction legitimately married to novel and exciting techniques of presentation, a combination which should bring us fresh and exciting entertainment superior to what we see and hear today." That was in 1953. Today, there seems little cause for hope from the present level where "science fiction" is indistinguishable from "horror," and "horror" from sadism. An audience for good science fiction films probably exists, but it is unlikely that producers will take that chance now. During the period when it seemed reasonable to expect some good SF films, the only chances that producers were willing to take with unfamiliar material were with material from contemporary life—"unfamiliar material" only in their previous films. With science fiction, everyone has followed the easy examples of a few successful horror films, in cheaper and cheaper productions that plagiarized their poverty of ideas and their antiscientific tone. Perhaps the problem of producing good SF films is more difficult than that of producing simply good films. Complex, individual, and intelligent films are rare, and films of this quality with unfamiliar, fantastic subjects are few indeed. *Things to Come, Caligari, Orpheus,* or *The Seventh Seal* are uncommon individual achievements; probably, good science fiction films will appear only in the form of such unusual achievements.[6] For the rest, if SF films continue to be produced, they will take the easy way of the scream instead of the statement, and continue to tell their increasingly irrational and vicious stories of impossible monsters, evil professors, and helpless victims. ("See a strip-teaser completely stripped—of flesh!" invites the latest poster.)

A possible explanation for the impossible, self-contradictory creatures and plots of these films is that their creators do not think it could matter to anyone: the monsters are unnatural—or unnaturalness—anyway, and the calculated response is "Quick! Kill it, before it reproduces!" (Poor André, poor Thing.) The assumption may be partially correct; and if many people like this sort of entertainment, the clear impossibility of creatures and plots may help ease the conscience. If the monsters are anything, they are evil conveniently objectified. But the "evils" that they represent, while sometimes pain and death, are just as often man's power, knowledge, and intelligence. Their part used to be played by the Devil or his demons. The destruction of the Things and of the mad scientists, and the senseless martyrdoms of the more rare "good" (if not "sane") scientists, resemble nothing so much as exorcism and the burning of witches and heretics.

Unfortunately, science fiction films have associated science, the future, the different, and the unknown with nothing but irrational fear. There are enough dangers; in these films the dangers are not natural, but impossible and monstrous—of the same character as those that one was believed to risk when, in another time, one forsook the True Faith for the Black Arts. What the equivalent of the Black Arts is imagined to be is often all too clear in each film. But the True Faith is never plainly shown, perhaps because if it is anything at all it is simply an absence of any thinking.

---

[6] Despite his success with *Beauty and the Beast,* Cocteau had trouble in obtaining backing for *Orpheus.*

Science and Fiction

by ADO KYROU

For all its liberating power, fantasy (in literature, and therefore also in film) has roots which go deep into theistic cultures and, more particularly, into theistic mythologies. The golem, symbol of a people's liberation, is born out of alchemical formulas; but alchemy, a Christian heresy that was a necessary revolt in its time, was really nothing but a cover for scientific experimenters and for Christians more intelligent than the orthodox. Frankenstein's monster, though untouched by the precepts of any theistic religion, except insofar as he distinguishes between good and evil, owes his existence to a fantastic science which can be traced back to traditional mythology. As for the many monsters, werewolves, cat women, and especially vampires of the screen, the peculiar power of the cinema may set them free from their ties with Christian mythology, but they still have all the characteristics of popular superstition: only with Matheson's superb *I Am Legend* is the poetry of vampires translated into a marvelous materialism. *I Am Legend,* however, is a book of science fiction (or, if you prefer, of scientific anticipation) and science fiction is materialistic by definition; what's more, it can cast off all ties with the culture of the past and steer a lone course into the glowing skies where poetry, freed from gravity, touches the real mysteries of matter, the wonders unknown to reality.

Invisibility, the plurality of worlds, the exploration of time and other dimensions, and the conversion of energy into matter are some of the major themes of science fiction, and in these and dozens of other vast fields, traditional habits of thought are no longer needed. Instead, the principles of modern science can be combined to generate speculative worlds in which humor, wonder, liberty—

From Positif 3, no. 24 (May 1957): 29–32. Reprinted by permission of Positif and the author.

in short, poetry—are given their head, devising new rules, inventing undreamed-of laws, and restoring man to his full dignity.

Science fiction films have no need of psychology, so it is only to be expected that they meet with contempt from the critics and even with supercilious smiles from enthusiasts of SF writing, whose favorite reaction is "But I don't go for *that* . . ."

True, the majority of SF filmmakers lack the insight of writers like Robert Sheckley, Fredric Brown, and Richard Matheson. Often the enthralling and liberating reaches of space are jarred by a reference to God or to some other entrenched concept which is equally false and ridiculous. But the plain fact remains that SF even at its most naive and puerile goes beyond ready-made ideas, reveals unsuspected possibilities, and opens up new vistas to even the most pedestrian mind. Clearly, what gives us so much hope in this (relatively) new mode of seeing and being, with its flights away from the familiar, its leaps into new lives, its thirst for richer experience, is that it is extraordinarily cinematic.

Two recent films offer fresh proof of that. It should not be forgotten, however, that they are to be viewed mainly as signposts to the future, as springboards to the glorious prophetic cinema which (since prophecy is in order) is bound to come some day.

The first of these films, Val Guest's *The Creeping Unknown* [*The Quatermass Experiment*], takes up the old theme of the monstrous individual who threatens the whole of mankind. Treated as pure SF, this well-worn theme becomes an ambitious excursion into speculative ideas. A form of life that preys on both plants and animals lodges in the body of a man who dared to enter its domain— space. Returning to earth with the amorphous alien inside him, the man becomes a means of transportation for his terrifying guest. Like a new breed of vampire, the creature absorbs ever-increasing quantities of plant and animal life, forcing the unfortunate carrier to kill in spite of himself. The monster's growth centers at first in the man's arm, which swells out of all proportion; then the carrier is absorbed entirely, and the monster appears as a slimy, tentacled mass that threatens to take over all the living things in the world.

Here, then, is a new approach to the monster theme, with the man becoming monstrous when invaded by an independent form of life. There is also a new approach to the stock ingredients of terror, thanks to a number of ideas which are both fascinating and disturbing: what frightens us is invisible (at least during the first part of the film); the possible catastrophe has no limits; and above all, the theme of "possession," given a fresh treatment with the help of such scientific ideas as symbiosis and parasitism, is developed into something far beyond childish stories about witches. In the past, possession was strictly a symbol of the opposition between good and evil; today no moral judgement can be made about either the possessor or the possessed. The fact is that normal standards are inadequate for measuring whatever is frighteningly alien or infinitely vast. Moreover, the scientist declares at the end of the film that he will start his experiments over again and send more men out into space: even though the earth may be endangered, he refuses to call a halt to "progress" and "knowledge."

For all that, the film suffers from being poorly made. Val Guest lacked the skill (or the means?) to make the most of the admirable final scene—the bloblike monster taking refuge in Westminster Abbey. Even so, the film marks a clear advance on its predecessors, thanks to the new ideas which shape its course.

There's also an admirable idea behind *Forbidden Planet*. The inhabitants of a distant world have developed their civilization to the extreme point of freeing themselves from matter, but in so doing they have let loose the unknown forces of the unconscious, which materialize as monsters.

Here the Christian concepts of the impalpable spirit and—by extension of the soul are turned inside out. This is another example of the way SF has changed the course of traditional fantasy, recharging an old idealistic myth with poetic materialism (or, if you prefer, romantic realism). There is no need to look back as far as Greek mythology to see how much progress has been made: compare *Forbidden Planet* with the eighteenth-century novel *The Devil in Love*, where Beelzebub materializes as a camel, and it is clear that the poetic charge has increased as the theistic symbolism has been drained away. Science has taken the place of magic circles; shifted in time and space, the fantastic adventures of the scholar whose subconscious escapes his control to create invisible but real monsters takes on extraordinary overtones.

While the theme in itself is intellectually stimulating, what makes me really enthusiastic is the way it is presented: the film contains all the basic elements of SF. These elements may be treated superficially, but they are always enthralling, since they point to new modes of thinking and being. Let us examine them briefly for their cinematic qualities:

1. *Space.* Since movement is the first and foremost element of the

cinema, we should not ignore the best reason there is for liking Westerns and adventure films. Vast plains crossed by hundreds of galloping horsemen, boundless oceans where ships sail toward a variety of dangers—these do not only take us on journeys but also invite us to live. If these spaces are transformed into space, the journey becomes immense and the invitation to live far more urgent. If a horseman alone in the desert is cinematic, then a flying saucer (or better, a spaceship) bound for unknown worlds at a speed faster than light is cinematic to an astronomical degree. Distances are no longer vast but cosmic, and movement within them becomes a new dimension.

2. *The machine.* One of the earliest films of Lumière was *The Sausage Machine.* The cinema, a machine itself, enabled the machine to acquire tremendous powers and to develop its possibilities in advance of scientific fact. On the screen, the machine loses its impersonal, inhuman, and mathematical nature and becomes a poetic object, very much in key with our modern idea of poetry. It is not surprising that the most dazzling poetic object of our age is the extraordinary machine of Marcel Duchamp, "The Bride Stripped Bare by Her Bachelors, Even"; and to a large extent the poetic qualities of Alfred Jarry, Raymond Roussel, and Kafka are due to the presence of that "modern" element, the machine.

What does it matter if the control panels, levers, rays, and robots are incomprehensible? Poetic materialization has no need of Cartesian logic. In *Forbidden Planet,* Robby the robot, the metal shutters which appear out of nowhere, and the mysterious means of transportation are all purely mechanical, and yet they create a magnificently strange environment which rejects soft curves in favor of straight lines, impressionism in favor of the hard edges of colossal modules. A new kind of life animates these machines, and while obeying man they reveal the menacing shadow of their revolt—or of their awakening consciousness.

3. *The new unknown.* By pushing the present-day possibilities of science to their furthest limits, SF draws us into a new kind of unknown—one which is not idealized but materialized in the extreme. In the past, the unknown was by definition something "different." Today, the unknown is the known with its potentialities developed to the point where it becomes mysterious. As the shell of the known is cracked, and sheer quantity becomes a change in quality, we enter not a different life but the fantastic mystery of our present life which we normally pass over.

On the screen, the most important elements of the new unknown are the settings. I referred earlier to the effects of space, and it is along these lines that the alien settings of SF are conceived. The designers of SF films—I am thinking particularly of *This Island Earth* and *Forbidden Planet*, but certainly not forgetting the great forerunner *Things to Come*—are the heirs of Gustave Doré, Max Ernst, and the illustrators of Jules Verne; they create new perspectives in which man is *forced* to behave differently, forgetting what our civilization has taught him. An open-minded viewer cannot remain unaffected by the monumental structures of *Forbidden Planet*. By contrast, the middle-class interiors of *Edward and Caroline* and *Behind the Mirror* can only seem banal and uninteresting.

4. *The new eroticism*. In the unknown realms of space, made accessible by the poetic intervention of the machine, people's behavior will change. Their interrelations will be different and, we hope, free. Of course, we may have some fear that the first tourists to land on Mars will take a bottle of wine and some sausage out of their picnic basket and settle down to discuss the concierge or the latest film of Bresson. Fortunately, the cinema has not (yet?) given us this dreary picture of new worlds being conquered. And in *Forbidden Planet*, efforts are made to present at least some new erotic possibilities. It goes without saying that these arise out of the costumes of the delightful Anne Francis. When her intergalactic fashions are displayed in the settings already described, the effects are extraordinary. Her short skirts, made by the robot servant, open the way to further erotic developments: there is no end to the new kinds of materials which might be invented, enabling women to dress and undress in unimagined ways.

A recurrent theme in the history of the cinema concerns a native woman who lives alone on an island, knowing nothing about sexual love until a man arrives to give her some lessons. (Examples include the films of Clara Bow and Dorothy Lamour, and even the Douglas Fairbanks *Mr. Robinson Crusoe*.) In *Forbidden Planet* (as, incidentally, in the W. C. Fields film *Never Give a Sucker an Even Break*) the theme is given a new lease on life by the nature of the girl: she has always lived alone with her father on a planet that is both wonderful and terrifying. She knows only a mechanical world, and when she discovers physical love she first makes use of machinery to win the man, then betrays everything she has been taught rather than betray her love. Here, the eternal theme of erotic revolt, breaking habits and family ties, is all the more moving because there are great physical and psychological dangers to be overcome. Yet a more spellbinding pair of lovers and a wilder passion can undoubtedly arise in SF cinema or writing and, by extension, in the people who see or read it.

I have made no mention of the humor to be found in SF, since it is still feeble on the screen even though excellent in Sheckley or Brown. There is no real humor in *Forbidden Planet;* but because the filmmakers are afraid to plunge the audience directly into the unknown there are several knowing winks, and these are irritating. Equally irritating are the allusions (brought in for the same reason) to familiar and false concepts of religion and the like. But although there is still a tremendous amount of progress to be made, today's SF films are a great source of hope, an exciting promise that we will go beyond the narrow bourgeois habits of thought.

Science Fiction's Museum
of the Imagination
by GUY GAUTHIER

Submarines, airplanes, artificial satellites, and moon rockets have all become familiar enough devices today, yet they existed already in the work of a nineteenth-century author who, for that reason, is one of the rare science fiction writers known to the general public—Jules Verne.

Verne neither invented nor influenced the invention of these products of modern technology. He dreamed about them, and he described his dreams. At the time, real scientists could very well have decried those dreams, but this would not have altered the fact that they were scientists and Verne was a poet. Bold hypotheses which may one day be proved right do not add up to a scientific mind. In fact, it is highly unlikely that a single gadget ever dreamed up by any science fiction writer could be made to work. If it were described in sufficient detail, nobody—except a mechanical maniac —would have the slightest interest in reading about it.

The writer can imagine the marvelous inventions of the future several decades in advance, but he can give them only a "poetic" existence. The less precise the scientific details, the more convincing the invention will be. The areas left hidden and unexplained are in fact essential to its nature as a literary creation. The writer is able to shift subtly to and fro between what is real and what is only suggested, between factual description and a vagueness which the reader will fill out with his own imaginings. The filmmaker is less fortunate: he must show the invention, and he must show it work-

From Image et Son, *May 1966, pp. 40–42, 44. Reprinted by permission of the Ligue Française d'Enseignement Permanente and the author.*

ing (though there *are* ways of preserving its mystery on the screen). A number of pitfalls lies in wait for anyone who sets out to turn a dream into pictures.

Captain Nemo's *Nautilus* is indeed the fictional ancestor of today's submarines. But in its own element, out in the open sea, it becomes a kind of fabulous creature, midway between a metal craft and a mythical monster. For Verne's contemporaries, it was an extension of the sea serpent rather than a foretaste of scientific progress. It takes its place in the ancient heritage of legend, and the story is much more concerned with the past than with the future.

That is why we accept, with an indulgent smile, the disparity between Captain Nemo's salon and the vessel which contains it. On the one hand there is an invention several decades in advance of the science of its time; on the other hand, a bourgeois interior which reflects not only the desire for comfort but also the aesthetic standards of that same time. Here we are up against one of the most frustrating paradoxes of science fiction: the artist's imagination can reach out ahead of science (within the limits already indicated) but not ahead of art, that is, ahead of itself. It was possible to predict artificial satellites almost a century before the fact; but nobody, even a short time before, could have predicted Picasso, Klee, or Kandinsky—except Picasso, Klee, and Kandinsky themselves. In science fiction, as a result, art museums of the future are left strangely empty. But that is not all. The aesthetic standards of an age are not reflected solely in its works of art; they also leave their mark, in some cases after a considerable lapse of time, on buildings and industrial products. Conversely, certain scientific requirements may create an aesthetic of industrial design which in turn influences artists. Thus the whole appearance of an age is conditioned by artistic concepts. The shape of a rocket, the outlines of a submarine, the look of a building made of glass and concrete—all these were more difficult to imagine than the idea of rockets, submarines, and skyscrapers.

The cinema suffers more from this fact than does literature. With a few impressive adjectives a writer can set the reader's imagination to work building a future dominated by old traditions and beliefs. The cinema must show and create. Of course, it too can sometimes limit itself to suggesting. The *Nautilus,* at the beginning of Richard Fleischer's *Twenty Thousand Leagues Under the Sea,* appears only as a luminous eye running just below the surface of the ocean on its way to sink ships. Here the dividing line between monster of the

deeps and technological marvel has not yet been drawn: the film is
still Jules Verne. Then the three survivors board the *Nautilus*,
which is shown in full detail. Here the disparity which can be
smiled at in Verne becomes more disturbing. The submarine is the
work of designers who are well aware of what modern craft of this
type look like, so that there is a compromise between the familiar
outline and the author's fantasies. Meanwhile, the salon remains
faithful to the ideals of a nineteenth-century bourgeois, and is
therefore out of place, poetically speaking, in the futuristic setting.

Science fiction writers are vaguely aware of this difficulty and try
to avoid it. They offer future worlds or far-off planets that are devoid of art—and yet are dominated by aesthetic ideas whose models
can easily be found in a textbook of cultural history. Sometimes a
writer may refer in passing to the existence of works of art, but he
is of very little help to a filmmaker trying to visualize them. Here
is an example from Ray Bradbury's *The Martian Chronicles:*
"Once they had liked painting pictures with chemical fire . . .
and talking into the dawn together by the blue phosphorous por-
traits in the speaking room." . . .

The disparity found in science fiction between technology and
aesthetics also extends to customs, morals, and emotions. An extreme
example is the Mu Empire in *Atarugon,* which follows barbaric
rites and customs yet wields formidable technological powers. More
common examples are the memories of olden times and nostalgia
for the Golden Age which crop up in spaceships headed for the
stars.

Not surprisingly, science fiction writers often choose to describe
worlds where art no longer exists. Societies ruled by machines and
robots, fascism triumphant, exhausted intellects, antlike organiza-
tions—these are favorite images of tomorrow's world. No art, no
books survive at the furthest journey of *The Time Machine;* art is
outlawed in *Alphaville* and *Fahrenheit 451.* It's possible that the
anxiety of our present age may offer a handy refuge for creative im-
potence. Undoubtedly, the pessimism of much science fiction is due
to the world we live in, a little more dehumanized day by day; but
in some cases it may arise simply as a matter of convenience. It is
easier to describe an ultramechanized universe, the end of the world,
or man's weaknesses carried to the extreme than it is to imagine
how a future society that is neither better nor worse than ours would
look and act. But fear of the future is as powerful a feeling as
nostalgia for the Golden Age. Only *La Jetée,* a science fiction mas-

terpiece, envisages a "peaceful" future, and even so gives no further
details—except that the hero, given the choice of living in it, pre-
fers the world of his childhood.

Too often science fiction does no more than project today's press-
ing concerns into the future or out among the stars. Literature, being more allusive than film, often has greater scope, but it is still
easy enough to tell not only the period when a story of the future
was written but also the ideology which inspired it.

As examples, consider two short stories: *Cor Serpentis* by Ivan
Yefremov and *First Contact* by Murray Leinster. Here, a Russian
and an American deal with the same theme: the first encounter between two different civilizations in space. In each story, the
encounter reveals the habits of one particular civilization and the
self-image that it wishes to present. I do not know what the first
cosmic encounter will be like, but I am quite sure it will be nothing
like Yefremov's or Leinster's.

To the extent that science fiction projects the present into the
future or into remote galaxies, it has a certain affinity with the philosophical fable; as Michel Butor has said, writers today often use
unknown planets in the same way as eighteenth-century writers
used Pacific islands. However, the aim is different. Science fiction
writers are not interested in turning out endless variations on the
voyage of Gagarin or in addressing thinly disguised moral messages
to their contemporaries. Their concern is to explore the present for
signposts to the future.

In this respect, Godard's approach in *Alphaville* was exemplary.
A science fiction story acted out in real locations could have been
a tremendous experience. Moreover, since the basic assumptions of
the story excluded any cultural environment, the risks were mini-
mized: there was no need to decide which of the kinds of art existing
today were destined to survive. This left only the far easier choice
of a technological environment.

Another novel idea behind the film was to take the dehumanized
world which everyone dreads and thrust into it a mythic figure carrying all the dreams of the collective unconscious. It would be an unexpected and marvelous irruption, like Judex appearing in a
nuclear research station, or Brick Bradford in an IBM plant—
mankind's ancient dreams challenging the automated future with
their explosive, liberating force. It would also put an end to the old
dispute between thought and action, reconciling Kafka and Verne,
Huxley and Wells, and making a happy marriage between philoso-

phy and the comic strip. In short, it would transcend genres and classifications.

Clearly, the film started out with brilliant ideas—and it would have taken genius to sustain them all the way through. Instead, Godard gave us the pitiful Eddie Constantine wandering like a lost soul amid pre-World War II pay phones and gas pumps and turn-of-the-century facades.

Another example of the same approach, but this time carried out with a firm and skillful hand, is Joseph Losey's *The Damned*. With uncompromising realism, it presents a world which belongs unmistakably to the time when it was made, yet in which men and children are preparing for an incredible future. A miniature mankind which can survive a nuclear holocaust is being taught all of our aberrations so that it will be able to repeat our mistakes. It has sometimes been denied that this film is science fiction, because it breaks away from the genre's standard (and often comforting) practice of extrapolating the present into the future. In *The Damned,* the future, and a grim one at that, is already amongst us.

A similar situation, less anguished because it derives from the lower-key theme of scientific discovery, is found in the Russian film of Mikhail Romm, *Nine Days of One Year*. This seems to be on the very border line of the genre. In judging it, however, we may easily be led astray by the term "science fiction," since the novelty of the science is not the only criterion. We are much more interested in what our emotions, attitudes, and ideas will be like in the age of future machines than we are in the machines themselves. In this area, as in the field of art, any long-term prediction is impossible, and so we may find that some of the most enterprising films are the closest to us in time and setting.

When dealing with the theme of imminent catastrophe, and the dread of a dehumanized future now taking shape, science fiction writers often choose to make a special exception in favor of works of art from the past, letting them survive as fragile messages from our dying humanism to future generations. As suggested earlier, this choice may be determined to a large extent by the impossibility of imagining the art forms of the future. All the same, it would be fascinating to know what works of art *would* survive.

Rightly or wrongly, I consider Chris Marker's *La Jetée* to be a masterpiece of science fiction—in fact, a masterpiece without qualification. The time paradox on which the film is based involves an interesting procedure. The hero is able to travel through time because of his obsession with a childhood memory. This is a familiar idea of Marker's: in *Sunday in Peking*, for example, he starts out by comparing the Avenue of the Mings to a book illustration remembered from childhood. The hero of *La Jetée* travels into the future through a network of lines making up a picture (somewhat reminiscent of Henri Michaux's drawings). This idea of traveling through a picture is an old favorite of cartoon animators. By using memories or works of art, science fiction enables us to explore a subjective universe. Anyone who first read Jules Verne in the old Hetzel editions cannot visualize the writer's universe independently of the illustrations of Riou, Benett, and Neuville. Some of these images remain vivid in our memory across the years, and they can easily send us, like the hero of *La Jetée*, on a journey backward in time. This is what happens in Karel Zeman's film based on Verne, *The Wonderful Invention*, in which live actors move through the familiar settings of the old engravings. These images, being charged with the emotions first aroused by Verne's stories, reflect our past dreams, creating a parallel universe of unsuspected richness.

In a more obvious way, when a contemporary work of art is projected into an imaginary future, it can become the symbol of our threatened values. Thus the rulers of the inhuman world of *Fahrenheit 451* single out books for attack, and it is a book, Eluard's *Capital of Pain*, which is featured as a clandestine object in *Alphaville*, where literature is banned. The authors naively assume that the cultural products of their time—or rather, of their civilization—are sacrosanct, and use them as unimpeachable tokens of so-called human values. Today there are doubts about science, and some of its basic assumptions are being challenged, yet as far as art is concerned people still take a more or less reverential attitude toward it; so that, paradoxically, it is easier to challenge Einstein than Shakespeare. In science fiction, it is easier to go from one point to another without passing through the space between, it is easier to travel in time or leap into hyperspace, than it is to question the value of Rimbaud's poetry or Cézanne's painting. We can accept the idea that such works of art may become outdated, but not—except in dire circumstances—forgotten.

Going back to *The Damned*, we find another aspect of the role of art in science fiction. Above the cave where the scientist is conducting his grotesque experiment in training the radioactive children, a woman creates strange sculptures which also, in their own way, point to the future. This prophetic quality of art has been used from time to time in science fiction, but rarely with such power. . . . Losey's film is outstanding because of the thoroughness with which he has carried out the aim described earlier—that is, examining the present for signs of what the future will be like, from the viewpoint not only of science but also of sociology, psychology, morals, and aesthetics. Here, I think, the tendencies of our present-day world have been extrapolated to their limits.

Although this survey of art in science fiction is necessarily incomplete, there is one important area which should not be, but too often is, ignored. Science fiction has to some extent taken over the themes, myths, and characters of a whole area of popular literature. It draws on a familiar mythology that has been built up by pulp serials, silent film serials, and comic strips. Thus it can give new life to adventure, to extravagance, to wild dreams, to everything that modern cinema and literature are starving to death. The imagery of *Flash Gordon* may still inspire some marvelous space operas which will carry us back to the planet Mongo in the same way as Karel Zeman carries us back into the Hetzel engravings. But the cinema will have to say goodbye to its grotesque papier-mâché monsters and find its way back to poetic fantasy. Spaceports will echo with the thunder of rockets, spaceships will meet amid the stars, and the Martian deserts will still have their mysteries. We will see Rimbaud's "pale crystalline skies," "fields of fire," and "pink and orange sands," and one day, perhaps, the screen will bring us the message from the inhabitants of *The Andromeda Nebula*.

Trieste: The First Science
Fiction Festival
by DARIO MOGNO

Articles about science fiction, which are no longer too rare even in Italy, nearly always start out by declaring that it is extremely difficult if not impossible to give a complete and foolproof definition of science fiction. They then invariably go on to give a definition—which is, of course, incomplete and unsatisfactory.

The trouble is that a definition can be complete only if it is prescriptive, like Jacques Bergier's; and he attaches so much importance to the validity of the scientific ideas involved that he has to exclude the works of such a well-known and highly admired writer as Ray Bradbury. More usually, definitions boil down to lists of themes on which the majority of science fiction stories are based. Besides the obvious difficulty of making such a list complete, it is also clear that no one can possibly think of all the legitimate science fiction themes which writers have not yet used.

In short, science fiction criticism today is going through the same stage as film criticism did with its theories of the "true nature" of the cinema. But science fiction, like the film, is a living, changing phenomenon that cannot be locked into fixed *a priori* categories. At the same time, just as it is wrong to define science fiction within such narrow terms that its best writers are excluded, one should not give such a broad definition that it embraces works which simply do not belong—as did the planners of the Trieste book and periodical exhibit, which included More's *Utopia,* Campanella's *City of the Sun,* and Kepler's *Somnium.*

From Bianco e Nero *24, no. 7–8 (July–August 1963): 96–109. Reprinted by permission of the publisher.*

While it is almost impossible to give a definition of science fiction as a literary genre, we should realize that a literary genre is not just an aesthetic category but also a reflection of psychological and socio-logical circumstances. It seems more useful to try to explain science fiction along these lines, in particular by considering its readers and the needs which they find satisfied by this branch of popular litera-ture. Science fiction writing reaches a public consisting of the regu-lar readers of specialized magazines. Therefore—and this is not an argument in a circle—science fiction is everything that is published in these magazines. While the readers look to the magazines to sat-isfy certain needs, the magazines depend on the readers for their existence, and their contents and style are influenced accordingly.

Just what needs *are* met by science fiction stories? A fully satisfac-tory answer could of course be given only by a thorough psychologi-cal study which would probe beneath all the rationalizations and bring the real motivations to light. But I think it is possible to ex-plore this field usefully with more rough and ready methods. It may be noted first of all that science fiction readers do not form a homo-geneous group but can be divided into at least two quite different subgroups. In the United States—which is both the homeland of sci-ence fiction and its biggest producer—these subgroups patronize different magazines. . . .

The distinction here is between "hot" and "cool" science fiction. The former includes all those stories which present "supercharac-ters" in spectacular situations (galactic wars, encounters with terrify-ing monsters, etc.). It is a kind of writing in which everything is larger than life. "Cool" science fiction, on the other hand, makes a plausible extrapolation of some current concern or phenomenon, setting it in the future so that certain features or tendencies in today's society can be emphasized, more often than not with an openly critical purpose. So-called "sociological" science fiction be-longs in this category. So do all stories which are based on logical paradoxes or on the negation or exaggeration of some scientific principle.

These then are the two major types of science fiction: to what needs do they correspond? . . . It seems reasonable to assume that the first type of science fiction does more than serve as a kind of es-cape literature. Because it revolves around "superheroes" who face and overcome "superobstacles" and "superenemies," this "hot" sci-ence fiction also lends itself to the psychological processes of pro-jection and identification. Through it, a certain kind of reader can satisfy ambitions and desires for power which are frustrated in his everyday life.

Except for stories based on logical paradoxes, which are simply intellectual games, the second type of science fiction raises more challenging questions. It would be particularly interesting to know what attracts readers to "sociological" science fiction, which has a smaller but better educated and more intellectual following than the other kinds. (The Italian edition of Galaxy, which has a circulation of 11,000, publishes stories almost exclusively of this type, and a survey made a few years ago showed that 80 percent of its readers are in the professional class.) What needs are satisfied by sociological science fiction, with its future societies of unbridled advertising and enslaved consumers, as in Frederik Pohl, or of world peace maintained by legalized killing, which performs the socially useful role of draining off man's aggressiveness, as in Robert Sheckley? Kingsley Amis, in New Maps of Hell, contends that the readers of this kind of science fiction are political progressives. If that is so—and I do not find it hard to believe—then science fiction, in criticizing reality from the outside, could very well appeal to the neurotic element in the kind of political progressive who can work for society only if he keeps it at arm's length. It is even possible that these stories have an ultimately conservative effect, like the political jokes of the Fascist era, which were said to be sanctioned by the regime because they provided a safety valve for discontent without threatening the existing order. The comparison is not as farfetched as it may seem, since many science fiction stories have a lot in common with political jokes: they present a problem by exaggerating its most obvious features, and offer no solution (this is invariably true of Pohl, who is considered the leading writer of sociological science fiction; the only exceptions I know of are some of John Wyndham's stories, such as "The Wheel"); and often they end abruptly, relying on a gimmick or twist (as in Fredric Brown's well-known "Sentry").

All this, of course, is simply to suggest that further study along these lines could lead to a more satisfactory definition of science fiction. Such a study could also explain more fully why the film has concentrated—and probably will continue to do so—almost entirely on the more popular but less interesting "hot" type of science fiction. In other words, it could reveal how this type of science fiction satisfies what must be a deeply rooted need in a large number of people. Being controlled by economic interests which require box-office successes, the film industry must appeal to a broad and undifferentiated public; it cannot undertake to produce films that will be appreciated only by a small minority. And all science fiction, but particularly the more intelligent, sociological kind, has developed a complex set of terms and conventions (rather like the political left, in fact) which can be understood only by its small number of regular readers.

For all that, the sociological branch of science fiction is certainly the most interesting, and it was probably with this in mind that Gastone Schiavotto, organizer of the First International Science Fiction Film Festival, approached the task of selecting the films to be shown. In point of fact, very little selection was involved, since only one of the films submitted was rejected. This was the Japanese-made *Gorath*, which was judged not to be science fiction, or at least to be only an inferior kind of science fiction, with a routine plot about monsters. Since this was the first festival of its kind, how-ever, a strong case could be made for displaying the widest possible range of films being produced in the science fiction genre, and on this basis I believe the Japanese film should have been accepted—especially as some of the films that did get shown were not science fiction either, and the overall quality was pretty low. . . . All kinds of science fiction were represented in the festival, with one excep-tion: there were no entries that fitted completely into the category of sociological science fiction. Some, however, were on the border line.

One such film was Oldrich Lipsky's *Muz z Prvniho Stolete (The Man from the Past)*, from Czechoslovakia. Though conceived as a satire, and ambiguous in outlook, it does to some extent examine the moral and social implications of a highly advanced technology. With a comic approach that is rather stagy and heavy-handed, the film relates the adventures of a twenty-first-century worker who acci-dentally finds himself on a spaceship bound for Earth in the twenty-fifth century. After an excellent beginning which recalls René Clair at his best, the film rapidly declines into a tedious moral tract. Milos Kopecky gives quite a good performance, but not good enough to save the film: his style is too obviously patterned on Chaplin's, with some gestures stolen outright. The ambiguity of the film stems from a conflict between the images and the dialogue. The former give a sympathetic view of the hero as he confronts the technologically ad-vanced and highly mechanized world of the twenty-fifth century, in which he finds little room left for the emotions, while the latter shows him up as petty and selfish compared to the people of the future, whose civilization is advanced not only scientifically but also on the moral plane.

The Polish animated cartoon *L'Amateur de Cybernétique* (*The Automation Nut*), directed by Stefan Szwakopf, is also in the satirical vein, but has a lighter—if not flippant—touch. A complex automated system which regulates the daily routine of a household breaks down, touching off a delightful series of witty and quickfire gags. These are, however, kept within the bounds of good taste, so that the film does not sink to the level of certain American cartoons—though neither does it rise to their technical polish.

This cartoon is simply an entertainment with no particular moral stand. Quite different is Jiri Trnka's *Kybernetica Babička* (*The Robot Grandmother*), from Czechoslovakia. With his brilliantly animated puppets, Trnka tells the story of a little girl who leaves the Earth, where she lives with her real-life grandmother, to try to find her parents on another planet, where she is put under the care of a "robot grandmother." Trnka's skill is too well known to need further praise, but I particularly admired the subtle effects, obtained largely through lighting and color, with which he suggests a whole range of different and complex expressions on the immobile faces of his puppets. He even succeeds in creating an expressive "face" for the robot grandmother, which is simply an armchair rolling about on casters and "speaking" with a cold, mechanical voice. Trnka gives this unusual robot more than mechanical coldness: its attitude toward the little girl is a mixture of contempt, derision, and outright hostility. Thus, behind the film's scarcely arguable thesis that no machine can ever replace the warmth of human affection, there are the glimmerings of what can only be called a reactionary idea—that the products of advancing science are in some obscure way hostile to man.

A similar idea can also be found in the Soviet *Chelovek Anfibya* (*The Amphibian Man*), directed by Terentev and Nemchenko, and the American *X: The Man with X-Ray Eyes*, directed by Roger Corman.

The idea comes across more clearly in the Soviet film, which openly borrows the theme and moral attitudes of Mary Shelley's *Frankenstein*. Adapted from a novel by Alexander Belyaev, the film has its science-fictional starting point in the creation of an amphibian man, a youth whose scientist father has given him the ability to live underwater as well as on land. But then, with a needlessly complicated plot, the film tells a banal story of the am-

phibian man's love for a young woman—a love that is thwarted
first by a cunning and greedy pearl fisher and then by the "monster's" own nature. Set in a South American country, the action of
the film is naive and full of inconsistencies: the makers get bogged
down in the tedious plot instead of exploring the psychological and
social implications of the amphibian man's condition. Just as Mary
Shelley's tale ends with the monster going mad and rebelling against
his creator, who is responsible for his misery, the Soviet film also
ends on a despairing note. The two lovers have to part, because
physiological changes in the amphibian man's body condemn him
to live underwater all the time; and the scientist expresses anguished regrets which amount to a warning that scientific research
should not try to overstep certain immutable bounds of nature.
While it is understandable that, more than a century ago, Mary
Shelley should have reacted against the facile optimism of the posi-
tivists and taken a gloomy view of certain lines of scientific development, it is not at all easy to see how the same attitude could arise
in the Soviet Union, which attaches such importance to scientific
research and is, in some areas, the most advanced country in the
world. This attitude may, of course, result from a reaction in certain intellectual circles against the official line; but in this instance,
at least, it marks a definite step backward, both in ideological and
in human terms.

A conclusion similar to that of *The Amphibian Man* is reached
in Corman's *X: The Man with X-Ray Eyes,* a film that is visually
impressive but artistically weak and perfunctory. A scientist, played
by Ray Milland with competence but not with the brilliance ac-
claimed by the newspaper reviewers, discovers a drug that increases
his visual powers, enabling him to see through the surface of objects to their internal structure. His colleagues do not believe him;
after accidentally killing one of them, he runs away and continues
his experiments secretly in a fairground side show, but is discovered
and has to go on the run again. He breaks the bank in a gambling
house, thanks to his ability to see through the backs of the cards
held by the other players, but by now he can no longer control the
changes in his eyes, which are transmitting unrecognizable images
of his surroundings. He ends up wandering into the middle of a
revivalist meeting, where he is execrated as a creature inspired by
the devil to transgress the limits that God has ordained for human
nature. Here, too, an opportunity has been thrown away. The film
starts out with a fascinating theme—the indifference and skepticism

which greet a discovery of potential benefit to mankind—and if
this had been developed, the result might have been a significant
work on the lines of Brecht's *Galileo*. Instead, the film opts for
medieval superstition, following a course that went out of favor
long ago in science fiction literature, especially among writers like
Asimov, Pohl, Sheckley, and Wyndham.

The misuse of a scientific discovery is also the pretext for another
American film, Bert I. Gordon's *Attack of the Puppet People*. Inflated with dime-store psychology, it tells the story of a pathologi-
cally lonely puppeteer who contrives to hold onto friends by reduc-
ing them to the size of dolls. The sole aim of the film is to exploit
the abnormal contrast in size between the miniaturized people and
the everyday objects around them—which was done much more
effectively years ago in Ernest B. Schoedsack's *Dr. Cyclops*. The
new film is so inferior and so insignificant that there is no point in
discussing it further.

The miniaturization of human beings (who in this case are also
immobilized) is the science-fictional ploy of a witty French film,
Pierre Kast's *Amour de Poche* (Pocket Love). This is the story of a
scientist who hides his mistress from the jealous vigilance of his
fiancée by making her small enough to carry in his pocket until he
can safely enlarge her again and make love to her. Though handled
with a brio and deftness typical of most French productions, the
film fails to rise above the level of a routine commercial feature.

Equally witty, and even more entertaining—though of no greater
artistic value—is Kast's other film, a short entitled *Monsieur
Robida, Prophète et Explorateur du Temps*. Through intelligent
use of camera movement and skillful editing, Kast succeeds in high-
lighting the weird and wonderful visions of this nineteenth-century
writer and illustrator, yet without forgoing the pleasure of gently
poking fun at Robida and the science fiction of his time. It is not
just a matter of chance that Kast has better success with a short
film than with a full-length feature. Like his "new wave" colleagues,
Kast came to filmmaking via the pages of *Cahiers du Cinéma* (to
which he used to be a contributor), and he approached it in an experimental spirit rather than with any profound need to express a
poetic or ideological world view. Thus his work is basically intel-
lectualized and sterile, and only in the narrow frame of a short film
is it redeemed by his technical skill and his sense of fantasy.

Like his *Cahiers* colleagues, Kast follows a style of criticism which
depends on somewhat arbitrary likes and dislikes, and I believe that

he was largely responsible for the uncritical enthusiasm lavished on another French short, Chris Marker's *La Jetée*. This enthusiasm even infected the jury—of which Kast was a member, thus being in a good position to make his views count. *La Jetée* takes place after World War III, when there is nuclear destruction everywhere and the few survivors have taken refuge in the tunnels of the Paris Métro. Here a scientist carries out an experiment in time travel, keying it to a man's vivid memory of a woman he met before the catastrophe. The experiment is a success, and the man travels back in time to the moment of his memory. In the hope that people in the past or future can provide drugs or other aid for the radiation-stricken survivors, the scientist keeps repeating the experiment. The man returns to the past to enjoy the company of the woman he loves, and the carefree atmosphere of these scenes makes a striking contrast with the tragic situation of the survivors in the Métro. In the end, the man decides to leave his own time for good and stay in the happy past; whereupon he dies—perhaps in deference to the science fiction principle that time travel is permissible only if it avoids the paradoxes resulting from an encounter between two different temporal versions of the same person. I have no fault to find with the science-fictional aspects of *La Jetée*, which could be taken as an interesting attempt to present the themes of time travel and its paradoxes in unconventional filmic terms. The distinctive feature of the film, which has led some reviewers to throw caution to the winds and acclaim it rapturously as a landmark in cinema history, is that it is composed of still images. The images are evocative, and while there is something rather mechanical about the way they are edited together, as if being made to fit a predetermined plan (especially in the contrast between past and present which is the keynote of the film), I do not deny that the execution is skillful and succeeds in creating dramatic situations of some expressive power. But this is a far cry from "an outstanding film in which the director has succeeded in conjuring up a new language." *La Jetée* seems to have touched off the same critical response as did *Hiroshima, Mon Amour:* in each case, an intellectual game has been mistaken for a new cinematic language, and an excessively literary form of dialogue, which fails to fuse with the images in a poetic whole, has been hailed as a sign of high art. It takes more than freezing movement within the frame to create a new language or a work of art, and while *La Jetée* holds one's interest, its true nature shows through all too clearly. This is a drawing-board exercise, planned and executed without any real contact with the sources of artistic creation —life and ideas.

A literary and pretentious text by Ray Bradbury—whose style is normally vigorous and effective, bordering on the poetic—serves as commentary to the banal and crudely colored art work of the American film, *Icarus, Montgolfier, Wright* by Julius Engel. This animated short gives a cursory review of the history of flight and ends with the hope that man will one day set out for the stars.

Pretentiousness is also the hallmark of the commentary of the Italian short, *The Origins of Science Fiction,* by Armando Silvestri and Cesare Falessi. Relying heavily on the spoken word rather than on the images—which consist of a poorly chosen and clumsily edited series of illustrations from science fiction books and magazines— the film tries unsuccessfully to trace the history of science fiction. The filmmakers' definition of science fiction is a restrictive one, rather like Bergier's: the only stories they recognize are those based strictly on foreseeable developments in science and technology. Their superficial and distorted view of science fiction prevents their film from having even a modest historical value.

The type of science fiction that Silvestri and Falessi place in the spotlight—while ignoring more interesting types, such as sociological science fiction—is well represented by an American film, John Wilson's *Journey of the Stars.* The documentary side of this is certainly well done, but in telling the story of an astronaut who sets out for the Andromeda Nebula it makes such repeated use of starfield backgrounds that it becomes boring.

More engrossing and visually more appealing is the Soviet documentary *Zvyezdnye Bratya (Brothers in Space),* directed by Bogopolev, which follows the cosmonauts Nikolayev and Popovich all the way from their preliminary tests and training through their space flight. Strictly speaking this is not science fiction at all; but the secrecy which has shrouded the Soviet space program gives the film a science fiction aura. Though efficiently made, the film suffers from the continual intrusion of heavy-handed propaganda, and this detracts from the genuine fascination of a documentary record that has never before been made public.

If the desire to compare the real-life progress of space flight with its imaginary counterpart in science fiction justifies the selection of the Soviet documentary, it is hard to see why the festival organizers included the English animated cartoon *Little Island,* by Richard Williams, which is pure fantasy. It tells the story of three little men,

symbolizing truth, beauty, and goodness, who meet on a desert island. Each of them goes through a series of transformations representing different aspects of his particular quality, and there is an
inevitable conflict among them which ends in total destruction.
With its fine technique and its imaginative pictorial style, *Little
Island* is certainly the best animated film at the festival, but its tor-
rent of sometimes baffling symbols and its basically abstract approach leave the viewer somewhat at a loss.

The other two English shorts are far inferior. These are John
Halas's mediocre *Moon Struck*, which uses animated paper dolls to
tell the story of two dogs going to the moon in search of a gigantic
bone, and Frank Tipper's pedestrian *The World of Little Ig,* an
animated cartoon in the worst Disney manner.

The two remaining films, Ernest Morris's *Masters of Venus*, from
Britain, and Jindrich Polak's *Ikarie XB 1,* from Czechoslovakia,
both deal with interplanetary travel, but with very different approaches and results.

Masters of Venus is not really a film at all but an assemblage of
eight episodes of a children's TV serial. It tells a naive and confused story of two children who accidentally travel to Venus, defeat
the Venusians, and thwart an attack on Earth. Made with the technical sobriety and polish found in most British films, *Masters of
Venus* is a typical example of what Kingsley Amis calls "space melodrama" and rightly describes as science fiction at its most immature.

In another class entirely is *Ikarie XB 1,* which is without doubt
the best film in the festival and a noteworthy achievement in its
own right. By avoiding the clichés of space travel—which, paradoxically, consist of extraordinary events—Polak creates a truly mature and accomplished film. Here, science fiction is not treated as a
pretext for a gratuitous show of tricks, as it usually is, but as a situation in which psychological and social problems can be explored—
in this case, the situation of forty men and women of different na-
tionalities living together in a spaceship as they travel in search of
a new world. The group has left Earth behind them to enter un-
charted regions of space, and with a fittingly slow and calm rhythm
the film tells the story of their long journey into the unknown. The
calm is broken only twice, by dramatic episodes which polarize the
fears, anxieties, and hopes of the small community.

Shortly after the spaceship has left Earth, while the astronauts
are still trying to adjust to their new situation, they come across a
derelict twentieth-century spacecraft whose crew was killed by a

weapon of war. Two men are sent out to explore the craft, and they find some atomic bombs which explode, killing both of them. The slow cutting of the sequence, and the almost total silence in which it unfolds, give this contact with the past the atmosphere of a ritual; they also prepare the viewer for its tragic ending, which comes across clearly as a deliberate moral comment on the folly of our age. This settling of accounts with the past marks the low point, both spatially and morally, in the ship's flight into the universe, which eventually leads the astronauts to a people of high civilization. The second episode, which comes near the end, fits into the same pattern, building up a tense and powerful climax not just for the sake of dramatic construction but because the whole conception of the film requires it to show the astronauts becoming aware of the value and meaning of their journey. For the climax is resolved when the spaceship—with a newborn baby crying aboard it—is approaching an inhabited world, and the astronauts realize that they will see that world only because its inhabitants have helped them, saving their lives.

This second episode concerns an astronaut who has been driven insane by exposure to atomic radiation. He brings into focus the doubts and anxieties of the whole crew, who are torn between fear of the unknown and the urge to explore, between acute nostalgia for their home planet and their awareness of being the spearhead of man's energies and aspirations. The episode is handled in a masterly fashion, like the encounter with the twentieth-century spacecraft— and, indeed, like all the other sequences leading up to it, which are just as important to the general architecture of the film. The excellent sets designed by Zazvorka contribute at least as much to the film's success as do the acting and photography. The environment he has created for the voyaging community is sober and sensible, yet he has also, as in the climactic sequence, managed to give it a remarkable expressive power (the metallic coldness and functional design of the long corridors through which the crazed astronaut wanders make a striking counterpoint to his emotional, irrational urge to return to his fellow men back on Earth).

The implied warning in the episode of the twentieth-century spacecraft; the communal life of people from different countries that are no longer divided into rival ideologies; and above all the ending, in which at one and the same time the astronauts recover from their crisis of helplessness and despair (the same crisis, by the way, which defeated the heroes of *The Amphibian Man* and *X: The*

Man with X-Ray Eyes) and the people of another world come to their aid, revealing a higher plane of kinship among civilized beings —all these help to make *Ikarie XB 1* a film of moral significance and great symbolic power. The film's makers have defined it as a twentieth-century science fiction drama, and the word drama aptly suggests both the breadth of its theme and the solidity of its construction. It deserved better company than the other films in competition at the first Trieste festival.

For all of us, and for the organizers, I hope that in future years the restrictive criteria applied this year will be abandoned and that the films selected will be larger in number, more interesting, of higher artistic quality, and above all more widely representative of the many directions in which the science fiction film is moving.

MOVING ON: THE 1960s AND AFTER

Filming THE TIME MACHINE
by DARRIN SCOT

. . . Photographing a story like *The Time Machine* was an interesting challenge to Director of Photography Paul Vogel—not only because it was loaded with problems of a mechanical nature, but because a certain correct psychological aura had to be created and maintained. The story is not fantasy, but science fiction—something that very possibly could happen when Man's knowledge of physics progresses a bit further. Therefore, everything that happened had to be visually believable. Whereas Vogel might have used fog filters or other obvious devices to suggest the exotic character of life on this planet 8,000 centuries hence, he wisely avoided them—and the result is much more credible.

The film begins, conventionally enough, in the Time Traveler's London home just at the turn of the century. The set is richly designed to the Victorian era with its wood-pannelled decor and rococo furnishings all done in lush warm tones. Vogel illuminated this set with amber light to paint up the mellow atmosphere of the period and to provide a strong visual contrast to the futuristic goings-on that were to follow. In moving into the future the technical problems increased accordingly.

For example, when the Time Traveler takes off through the fourth dimension, his machine is located in his laboratory. Since the roof of the room is mainly open skylight, the light or darkness outside sets the lighting key for the scene. As the Traveler whirls faster and faster through Time, this lighting key must change accordingly.

In order to simulate such an effect, Vogel had huge circular shutters built and mounted in front of each "brute" arc used to light the scene. These discs, roughly seven feet in diameter, were divided

From American Cinematographer *41, no. 8 (1960): 491–98. Reprinted* by permission of the publisher.

into four segments like a pie. One segment was left clear to indicate daylight, another had a pink gelatin (#14) to indicate sunrise, another had an amber gelatin (MT-2) to indicate evening, and a fourth had a blue gelatin (#25) to indicate night. As each day flew by in a matter of seconds these discs were turned by hand from below by means of a chain and gear arrangement. Simultaneously the arcs were raised and lowered by means of see-saw devices to contrast the *high light* of midday with the *low* light of evening. Arcs illuminating the backing outside the window were alternately masked by mechanically-operated flat shutters synchronized with the discs.

In the sequence where the Traveler speeded up the machine so that each day became a mere flicker, Vogel had the circular shutters converted so they were composed of alternating black-and-white segments only. The shots through the skylight showing the rapidly changing conditions outside were accomplished later by means of special-effects animation to coincide with the changing light on the set.

Aside from the main challenge of synchronizing all of the discs, shutters, and see-saws so that a uniform result would be produced, there was the problem of balancing the light intensities as they were transmitted by the different colored gelatins, so a consistent exposure could be maintained. For example, the blue gelatin transmitted only one-quarter the amount of light passed by the clear segment. To equalize exposure, the pink and amber gelatins were doubled in thickness and white gauze was placed over the clear areas.

Creating these lighting effects right on the set not only produced a much more realistic result, but saved thousands of dollars which otherwise would have been spent to produce a similar effect by means of optical printing.

As the Traveler is entombed by the lava flow—presumably for thousands of centuries of rushing time—he is seen against a background of huge rocks piled around his Time Machine. The sequence was shot against a solid blue backing to permit double printing of the rock background. As the erosion of time gradually liberates him, the rock background melts away by means of animation. However, the rocks piled about the machine were the real thing, and these had to be pulled out of the way precisely on cue by means of concealed wires.

As the Time Traveler makes brief stops along the way in his flight through time, the changes in his physical surroundings had to be made apparent. In his laboratory this was done by gradually aging the set until it seemed actually to fall apart in ruin. The street outside his home proved more of a problem, since a large area had to change radically in character through the ages. This was accomplished by photographing several scenes in a variety of locales, then combining them as traveling mattes to form a single composition. Although the resulting composite was produced through optical printing, the several scenes involved had to match exactly in photographic character in order to produce a realistic blend.

The sequences showing life 8,000 centuries in the future called for a strong photographic contrast between the aboveground world of the Eloi and the underground domain of the dreadful Morlocks. In shooting the lush Eden of the Eloi, Vogel kept the illumination bright and relatively flat by using a front light source. The result enhances the almost two-dimensional character of the docile Eloi moving about their never-never land in a semidream state.

The Morlocks, on the other hand, were shadowy, sinister creatures who were never, at any time, to be shown too clearly. They are first seen only as patches of luminous gray-green darting about the shadows of the night foliage. Later, in their underground habitat, we see them a bit more clearly, but they are kept shadowy—not only to preserve the horror of the unknown, but to prevent the details of their elaborate makeup from becoming too obvious. . . .

The Time Machine, although made on a relatively low budget, is not only absorbing entertainment, but a technical accomplishment of no small proportions and an excellent example of lighting and photographic innovation.

From "The Journal of FAHRENHEIT 451"
by FRANÇOIS TRUFFAUT

WEDNESDAY, FEBRUARY 2 [1966]

. . . We move into Montag's house. The set is not very well done. Instead of the stark ancient-and-modern contrasts I was hoping for, there's simply a rather well-to-do middle-class interior with a big television screen on the wall and only those details that I specifically asked for—three antique telephones, automatic doors, a big spyhole lens in the door, and a Breton coffee service. I quickly make some changes in the furniture and rearrange the smaller props, but for the rest it's too late. In making a film, it's sometimes better not to be too trusting.

THURSDAY, FEBRUARY 3

The scenes planned for this set are lengthy ones with a mobile camera, so I hope to get back on schedule or at least avoid falling further behind. But the lengthy scenes involve projections on the television screen, and these can't always be done quickly. To serve as interludes between the television programs, I had some footage shot of kaleidoscope images, and a second projector is synchronized with the main projector and the camera so that these images can be dissolved in and out at the right time. Since the two projectors have to start running at the same time, there has to be extra leader on the kaleidoscope footage. The Technicolor people forgot to put this

From Cahiers du Cinéma, nos. 176, 177, 178, 180 (1966). Copyright © 1966 by Les Éditions de l'Étoile. Reprinted by permission of Les Éditions de l'Étoile and Grove Press, Inc.

on, so it's done in our cutting room. Unfortunately, the projector won't take the splices. So we lose two hours . . .

TUESDAY, FEBRUARY 8

Only two scenes today, but both of them difficult for the camera crew.

First scene: Montag comes home, takes off his uniform in the hall, looks into the living room where the TV screen is switched on but blank, calls Linda, goes into the kitchen, comes out again, then sees Linda lying unconscious in the bathroom. Dolly and zoom. He reenters the frame, lifts Linda up and carries her to the bed. A running time of 50 seconds with 11 focus changes. This and the following scene are shot with an Italian device called the Elemak, a sort of tripod mounted on four wheels which can be turned in any direction by a small vertical steering wheel. The operator, focus-puller, and assistant follow the machine on foot, keeping alongside or behind. It's a sort of compromise between the camera dolly and the hand camera, extremely practical.

Second scene, continuation of the first: Montag puts Linda down on the bed, unfastens the top of her dress, runs to the telephone in the hall, calls the hospital, dashes to switch off the TV, goes to a second telephone in the bathroom to report on the kind of pills his wife has taken, then returns to the bedroom and the third phone, and the scene ends on the still unconscious Linda. Running time, 1 minute 40 seconds; 16 changes of focus. Several times the camera crew bumps into a wall or makes a bad turn, and in one take the TV projection isn't switched on at the right time; but finally the fifth take goes well all the way through . . .

SATURDAY, FEBRUARY 19

. . . Two months ago *Fahrenheit 451,* in script form, was a hard and violent film, inspired by worthy sentiments and altogether on the serious side. In shooting it, I realize that I have been trying to give it a lighter tone. As a result, I have been viewing the script with a certain detachment, treating the future in the same way as I treated the past in *Jules and Jim*—not trying to ram it down the audience's throat or make them believe in it too deeply. If I had to start the film over, this is what I'd say to the art director, costume designer, and cinematographer by way of instructions: "Let's make a film about life as children see it, with the firemen as toy soldiers, the firehouse as a model, and so on." I don't want *Fahrenheit 451* to look like a Yugoslav film or a left-wing American film. Despite its "big theme," I'd like to keep it unpretentious, a simple film . . .

WEDNESDAY, FEBRUARY 23

Montag and Clarisse arrive at the basement cafe in the firehouse building. Clarisse phones the Captain, posing as Mrs. Montag: "My husband is ill in bed, and he won't be in today." It's a childish scene right out of *The 400 Blows,* and I like it because it has a matter-of-fact simplicity which is unexpected in a science fiction context.

To tell the truth, *Fahrenheit 451* will disappoint fantasy lovers because it is science fiction in the style of *The Umbrellas of Cherbourg.* That was an ordinary story with a simple twist: everyone sings instead of speaking. *Fahrenheit 451* is an ordinary story in which everyone is forbidden to read . . .

TUESDAY, MARCH 1

Interior of the monorail which Montag rides to work every day and in which he is "picked up" by Clarisse. Ever since the script was written I've preferred the character of Linda, conventional but touching, to that of Clarisse, more heavily conventional because pseudo-poetic. You may wonder why I'm knowingly filming two conventional roles. The answer is that any film script involves advantages and disadvantages, or rather that any basic decision about a script means that something is deliberately sacrificed. If a filmmaker decides to plunge into science fiction, then he sacrifices psychology and a sense of real life; but this is not too important if he can make up for them in plausibility and lyricism. In other words, I think that before starting on a film one has to decide what tracks to drive it along. It isn't possible either to avoid making this choice or to switch tracks after the film is under way.

The fact remains that I have desexed Clarisse to avoid involving her and Montag in the kind of adulterous situation which has had a thorough workout in fields outside science fiction. Clarisse is neither a mistress, nor a girl scout, nor a girlfriend; she is simply a young woman full of awkward questions who appears on Montag's path and leads him away from it. Julie Christie gives her the necessary reality and I don't worry too much more about the character . . .

WEDNESDAY, MARCH 16

Exteriors of Montag's house. The first time he comes home; the scene where he goes out and is followed by Clarisse; the scene where Linda goes out on her way to denounce him; and the scene where the fire truck stops and he exclaims, "But that's my house!"

In order to film these 12 miserable shots before 4 P.M., when it will be too dark, there has to be a procession rather like the picnic in *Citizen Kane*. A bus brings 30 extras that I don't need. One truck carries artificial hedges to mask any unwanted details in the location, while another is loaded with squares of real turf. There's the sound truck, the car with camera mount, the refreshment bus, the lighting truck, the camera truck, and so on. Even the fire truck is carried in its own special truck. The four leads each have their stand-ins, and two of the leads bring their own trailers for making up.

In the studio I can forget about these 65 people who work around the camera, but here I see them and feel their presence, and I think of how I filmed *Les Mistons* with only cameraman Jean Malige and my friends Claude de Givray and Robert Lachenay at my side.

Here we're caught in the machinery of a big budget (about 1.5 million dollars), with money being thrown away on things which don't show on the screen. For example, while there are few technological devices in the film, there are about thirty important objects —and not one of them has been really well designed or executed, for lack of inventiveness and money . . .

WEDNESDAY, MAY 18

Pinewood—We've finished editing the last third of the film and with Thom Noble [the editor] we're now concentrating on the fine cutting of the first eight reels. The running time has been reduced

from 118 minutes to 113, but we still haven't reached the 110 that
I wanted. Those three extra minutes will be the hardest to cut. The
dialogue scenes are already tight, and I make it a rule not to en-
croach on the "privileged moments," meaning the purely visual
scenes—the firemen dashing to and fro, the truck answering a call,
fires, and various odds and ends.

We're going to try replacing the usual fade-outs with "white-outs"
—making the scenes go white instead of black. This will give more
of a science fiction effect, but the trouble is that after the release
prints have been projected for a few days, the inevitable scratches
will show up much more noticeably on white. Since the same kind
of thing happens with the framing and the sound track, which are
botched up in theaters all over the world, even in Los Angeles, I
think it's better to work for the first screening and not worry about
what happens later. In *La Religieuse,* Jacques Rivette replaced the
fades and dissolves with short lengths of black leader, inserting them
as straight cuts to keep the scenes intact. I'm going to borrow
Rivette's idea and cut in strips of different colors here and there—
fire-truck red in one place, flame-yellow in another . . .

THURSDAY, MAY 26

First session with Bernard Herrmann. We view the film reel by
reel, discussing each one before going on to the next . . . Music
will play an important and lengthy part in the film, but it is agreed
with Bernard Herrmann that his score should not have any meaning.
If *Fahrenheit 451* is a commercial failure, we're not relying on the
music to help save it. The sole function of the music is to highlight
the strangeness of the scenes. Nothing sentimental with Montag and
Clarisse, nothing sinister with the Captain, no comic or even light-
hearted effects—instead, it will be *intriguing* music. For the book-
burning scenes it will be barbaric and primitive, while for the other
scenes involving books it will be a mixture of old and modern
styles. Right away we rejected the idea of concrete or electronic
music, or any of the futuristic clichés and repetitive effects which
TV, both in Europe and the United States, plunges blindly into at
every opportunity.

Filming 2001: A SPACE ODYSSEY
by HERB A. LIGHTMAN

. . . I had heard about the elaborate "command post" which had been set up at Borehamwood during the production of *2001*. It was described to me as a huge, throbbing nerve center of a place with much the same frenetic atmosphere as a Cape Kennedy block-house during the final stages of countdown.

"It was a novel thing for me to have such a complicated information-handling operation going, but it was absolutely essential for keeping track of the thousands of technical details involved," Kubrick explained. "We figured that there would be 205 effects scenes in the picture and that each of these would require an average of ten major steps to complete. I define a 'major step' as one in which the scene is handled by another technician or department. We found that it was so complicated to keep track of all of these scenes and the separate steps involved in each that we wound up with a three-man sort of 'operations room' in which every wall was covered with swing-out charts including a shot history for each scene. Every separate element and step was recorded on this history—information as to shooting dates, exposure, mechanical processes, special requirements, and the technicians and departments involved. Figuring ten steps for 200 scenes equals 2,000 steps—but when you realize that most of these steps had to be done over eight or nine times to make sure they were perfect, the true total is more like 16,000 separate steps. It took an incredible number of diagrams, flow charts, and other data to keep everything organized and to be able to retrieve information that somebody might need about something someone else had done seven months earlier. We had to be able to tell which stage each scene was in at any given moment—and the system worked."

From American Cinematographer *49, no. 6 (1968): 442–47. Reprinted by permission of the publisher.*

THE IDEAL OF THE "SINGLE-GENERATION LOOK"

A film technician watching *2001* cannot help but be impressed by the fact that the complex effects scenes have an unusually sharp, crisp, and grainfree appearance—a clean "single-generation look," to coin a phrase. This is especially remarkable when one stops to consider how many separate elements had to be involved in compositing some of the more intricate scenes.

This circumstance is not accidental, but rather the result of a deliberate effort on Kubrick's part to have each scene look as much like "original" footage as possible. In following this pursuit he automatically ruled out process shots, ordinary traveling matte shots, blue-backings, and most of the more conventional methods of optical printing.

"We purposely did all of our duping with black and white, three-color separation masters," he points out. "There were no color interpositives used for combining the shots, and I think this is principally responsible for the lack of grain and the high degree of photographic quality we were able to maintain. More than half of the shots in the picture are dupes, but I don't think the average viewer would know it. Our separations were made, of course, from the original color negative and we then used a number of bipack camera-printers for combining the material. A piece of color negative ran through the gate while, contact printed onto it, actually in the camera, were the color separations, each of which was run through in turn. The camera lens 'saw' a big white printing field used as the exposure source. It was literally just a method of contact printing. We used no conventional traveling mattes at all, because I feel that it is impossible to get original-looking quality with traveling mattes."

SMOOTH TRIPS FOR STAR-VOYAGERS

A recurring problem arose from the fact that most of the outer-space action had to take place against a star-field background. It is obvious that as space vehicles and tumbling astronauts moved in front of these stars they would have to "go out" and "come back on" at the right times—a simple matter if conventional traveling mattes were used. But how to do it a better way?

The better way involved shooting the foreground action and then making a 70 mm print of it with a superimposed registration grid and an identifying frame number printed onto each frame. The grid used corresponded with an identical grid inscribed on animation-type platens.

Twenty enlargers operated by twenty girls were set up in a room and each girl was given a five- or six-foot segment of the scene. She would place one frame at a time in the enlarger, line up the grid on the frame with the grid on her platen, and then trace an outline of the foreground subject onto an animation cel. In another department the area enclosed by the outline would be filled in with solid black paint.

The cels would then be photographed in order on the animation stand to produce an opaque matte of the foreground action. The moving star background would also be shot on the animation stand, after which both the stars and the matte would be delivered to Technicolor Ltd. for the optical printing of a matted master with star background. Very often there were several foreground elements, which meant that the matting process had to be repeated for each separate element.

THE MECHANICAL MONSTER WITH THE DELICATE TOUCH

In creating many of the effects, especially those involving miniature models of the various spacecraft, it was usually necessary to make multiple repeat takes that were absolutely identical in terms of camera movement. For this purpose a camera animating device was constructed with a heavy worm gear twenty feet in length. The large size of this worm gear enabled the camera mount of the device to be moved with precise accuracy. A motorized head permitted tilting and panning in all directions. All of these functions were tied together with selsyn motors so that moves could be repeated as often as necessary in perfect registration.

For example, let us assume that a certain scene involved a flyby of a spaceship with miniature projection of the interior action visible through the window. The required moves would be programmed out in advance for the camera animating device. A shot would then be made of the spaceship miniature with the exterior properly lighted, but with the window area blacked out. Then the film would be wound back in the camera to its sync frame and another identical pass would be made. This time, however, the exterior of the spacecraft would be covered with black velvet and a scene of the interior action would be front-projected onto a glossy white card exactly filling the window area. Because of the precision made possible by the large worm gear and the selsyn motors, this exact dual maneuver could be repeated as many times as necessary. The two elements of the scene would be exposed together in perfect registration onto the same original piece of negative with all of the moves duplicated and no camera jiggle.

Often, for a scene such as that previously described, several elements would be photographed onto held-takes photographed several months apart. Since light in space originates from a sharp single point source, it was necessary to take great pains to make sure that the light sources falling on the separate elements would match exactly for angle and intensity.

Also, since the elements were being photographed onto the same strip of original negative, it was essential that all exposures be matched precisely. If one of them was off, there would be no way to correct it without throwing the others off. In order to guard against this variation in exposure very precise wedge-testing was made of each element, and the wedges were very carefully selected for color and density. But even with all of these precautions there was a high failure rate and many of the scenes had to be redone.

"We coined a new phrase and began to call these 'redon'ts,'" says Kubrick, with a certain postoperative amusement. "This refers to a redo in which you don't make the same mistake you made before."

FILMING THE ULTIMATE IN SLOW MOTION

In the filming of the spacecraft miniatures, two problems were encountered which necessitated the shooting of scenes at extremely slow frame rates. First, there was the matter of depth-of-field. In order to hold both the forward and rear extremities of the spacecraft models in sharp focus, so that they would look like full-sized vehicles and not miniatures, it was necessary to stop the aperture of the lens down to practically a pinhole. The obvious solution of using more light was not feasible because it was necessary to maintain the illusion of a single bright point light source. Secondly, in order to get doors, ports, and other movable parts of the miniatures to operate smoothly and on a "large" scale, the motors driving these mechanisms were geared down so far that the actual motion, frame by frame, was imperceptible.

"It was like watching the hour hand of a clock," says Kubrick. "We shot most of these scenes using slow exposures of four seconds per frame, and if you were standing on the stage you would not see anything moving. Even the giant space station that rotated at a good rate on the screen seemed to be standing still during the actual photography of its scenes. For some shots, such as those in which doors opened and closed on the spaceships, a door would move only about four inches during the course of the scene, but it would take five hours to shoot that movement. You could never see unsteady movement, if there was unsteadiness, until you saw the scene on the screen—and even then the engineers could never be sure exactly where the unsteadiness had occurred. They could only guess by looking at the scene. This type of thing involved endless trial and error, but the final results are a tribute to MGM's great precision machine shop in England."

IT'S ALL DONE WITH WIRES—BUT YOU CAN'T SEE THEM

Scenes of the astronauts floating weightlessly in space outside the *Discovery*—and especially those showing Gary Lockwood tumbling off into infinity after he has been murdered by the vengeful computer—required some very tricky maneuvering.

For one thing, Kubrick was determined that none of the wires supporting the actors and stunt men would show. Accordingly, he had the ceiling of the entire stage draped with black velvet, mounted the camera vertically, and photographed the astronauts from below so that their own bodies would hide the wires.

"We established different positions on their bodies for a hip harness, a high-back harness, and a low-back harness," he explains, "so that no matter how they were spinning or turning on this rig —whether feetfirst, headfirst or profile—they would always cover their wires and not get fouled up in them. For the sequence in which the one-man pod picks Lockwood up in its arms and crushes him, we were shooting straight up from under him. He was suspended by wires from a track in the ceiling and the camera followed him, keeping him in the same position in the frame as it tracked him into the arms of the pod. The pod was suspended from the ceiling also, hanging on its side from a tubular frame. The effect on the screen is that the pod moves horizontally into the frame to attack him, whereas he was actually moving toward the pod."

To shoot the scene in which the dead astronaut goes spinning off to become a pinpoint in space took a bit of doing. "If we had actually started in close to a six-foot man and then pulled the camera back until he was a speck, we would have had to track back about 2,000 feet—obviously impractical," Kubrick points out. "Instead we photographed him on 65 mm film simply tumbling about in full frame. Then we front-projected a six-inch image of this scene onto a glossy white card suspended against black velvet and, using our worm gear arrangement, tracked the camera away from the miniature screen until the astronaut became so small in the frame that he virtually disappeared. Since we were rephotographing an extremely small image there was no grain problem and he remained sharp and clear all the way to infinity."

The same basic technique was used in the sequence during which the surviving astronaut, locked out of the mother ship by the computer, decides to pop the explosive bolts on his one-man pod and blast himself through the vacuum of space into the air lock. The air-lock set, which appears to be horizontal on the screen, was actually built vertically so that the camera could shoot straight up through it and the astronaut would cover with his body the wires suspending him.

First a shot was made of the door alone, showing just the explosion. Then an undercranked shot of the astronaut was made with him being lowered toward the camera at a frame rate which made him appear to come hurtling horizontally straight into the lens. The following shot was overcranked as he recovered and appeared to float lazily in the air lock.

A FASCINATING FERRIS WHEEL

2001: A Space Odyssey abounds in unusual settings, but perhaps the most exotic of them all is the giant centrifuge which serves as the main compartment of the *Discovery* spacecraft and is, we are told, an accurate representation of the type of device that will be used to create artificial gravity for overcoming weightlessness during future deep-space voyages.

Costing $750,000, the space-going "ferris wheel" was built by the Vickers-Armstrong Engineering Group. It was thirty-eight feet in diameter and about ten feet in width at its widest point. It rotated at a maximum speed of three miles per hour and had built into it desks, consoles, bunks for the astronauts, and tomblike containers for their hibernating companions.

All of the lighting units, as well as the rear projectors used to flash readouts onto the console scopes, had to be firmly fixed to the centrifuge structure and be capable of functioning while moving in a 360° circle. The magazine mechanisms of the Super-Panavision cameras had to be specially modified by Panavision to operate efficiently even when the cameras were upside down.

"There were basically two types of camera setups used inside the centrifuge," Kubrick explains. "In the first type the camera was mounted stationary to the set, so that when the set rotated in a 360° arc, the camera went right along with it. However, in terms of visual orientation, the camera didn't 'know' it was moving. In other words, on the screen it appears that the camera is standing still, while the actor walks away from it, up the wall, around the top, and down the other side. In the second type of shot the camera, mounted on a miniature dolly, stayed with the actor at the bottom while the whole set moved past him. This was not as simple as it sounds because, due to the fact that the camera had to maintain some distance from the actor, it was necessary to position it about twenty feet up the wall—and have it stay in that position as the set rotated. This was accomplished by means of a steel cable from the outside which connected with the camera through a slot in the center of the floor and ran around the entire centrifuge. The slot was concealed by rubber mats that fell back into place as soon as the cable passed them."

Kubrick directed the action of these sequences from outside by watching a closed-circuit monitor relaying a picture from a small vidicon camera mounted next to the film camera inside the centrifuge. Of the specific lighting problems that had to be solved, he says:

"It took a lot of careful preplanning with the Lighting Cameraman, Geoffrey Unsworth, and Production Designer Tony Masters to devise lighting that would look natural, and, at the same time, do the job photographically. All of the lighting for the scenes inside the centrifuge came from strip lights along the walls. Some of the units were concealed in coves, but others could be seen when the camera angle was wide enough. It was difficult for the cameraman to get enough light inside the centrifuge and he had to shoot with his lens wide open practically all of the time."

Cinematographer Unsworth used an unusual approach toward achieving his light balance and arriving at the correct exposure. He employed a Polaroid camera loaded with ASA 200 black-and-white film (because the color emulsion isn't consistent enough) to make still photographs of each new setup prior to filming the scene. He found this to be a very rapid and effective way of getting an instant check on exposure and light balance. He was working at the toe end of the film latitude scale much of the time, shooting in scatter light and straight into exposed practical fixtures. The 10,000 Polaroid shots taken during production helped him considerably in coping with these problems.

"FILMMAKING" IN THE PUREST SENSE OF THE TERM

To say that *2001: A Space Odyssey* is a spectacular piece of entertainment, as well as a technical tour de force, is certainly true, but there is considerably more to it than that.

In its larger dimension, the production may be regarded as a prime example of the *auteur* approach to filmmaking—a concept in which a single creative artist is, in the fullest sense of the word, the author of the film. In this case, there is not the slightest doubt that Stanley Kubrick is that author. It is *his* film. On every 70mm frame his imagination, his technical skill, his taste, and his creative artistry are evident. Yet he is the first to insist that the result is a group effort (as every film must be) and to give full credit to the 106 skilled and dedicated craftsmen who worked closely with him for periods of up to four years.

Among those he especially lauds are: screenplay coauthor Arthur C. Clarke, Cinematographers Geoffrey Unsworth and John Alcott, and Production Designers Tony Masters, Harry Lange, and Ernie Archer. He also extends lavish praise to Special Effects Supervisors Wally Veevers, Douglas Trumbull, Con Pederson, and Tom Howard. . . .

The Odyssey of Stanley Kubrick:
Part 3: Toward the Infinite—2001
by MICHEL CIMENT

"Eternity is in love with the productions of time."

—WILLIAM BLAKE

Creating a utopia involves an intellectual game, a vertiginous calculation which was bound to attract Kubrick. And setting a story in 2001 [1] would mean going beyond the collapsing civilization of which he had until now chosen to give such a dark picture. Aurel David has shown that "the balance between the living and lifeless parts of the world has now been upset by a continual loss of the living substance. Life is leaking from the biologist's hands into the physicist's." [2] The aim of cybernetics is to replace man with machinery for all routine work, for all operations that are mechanical and intermediary. While it may not be able to touch the human part of man, it can take over or destroy—perhaps to the last 0.01 percent—the part that is inhuman and replaceable by technology, the intellect. Man could then be fully mechanized, and would no longer be man. Aurel David notes that those involved in hunting down the last refuges of life seem to take pleasure in misfortune; they betray a romantic pessimism, very much in tune with the times, which is well expressed by the great cybernetician Norbert Wiener: "We are castaways on a doomed planet."

From Positif, *no. 98 (1968): 14–20. Reprinted by permission of* Positif *and the author.*

[1] Part of Ray Bradbury's *Martian Chronicles* is set in 2001, as is Arno Schmidt's *Republic of Scientists,* a satire about the world that follows an era of happy teen-agers.

[2] Aurel David, *La Cybernétique et l'Humain.*

Cybernetics was bound to fascinate Kubrick, with his passionate interest in the way human actions can be controlled and living beings can be mechanized. The word (from the Greek *kubernesis,* "pilot") had already been used by Ampère with reference to politics, so that it forms a link between the mechanisms of power analyzed by Kubrick in his previous films and the futuristic science of *2001.* But this control, no matter how efficient, is powerless to determine the purpose of man's actions. Here man is on his own, and the machine can do nothing. That is what *2001* shows us. Here again we find Kubrick's anguish in the face of the primal question raised by Pascal's freethinker: "By whose order and command have this place and time been assigned to me?" The anthropomorphic view of ancient and Renaissance times gave way to the reign of science, which relegated man to his proper place in the universe but still aimed to overcome all the obstacles of nature, so that nineteenth-century man even had the wild dream of attaining absolute knowledge. But modern science has shown that we can no longer look upon nature as a thing in itself, as an ultimate objective reality. "The subject of research is therefore no longer nature in itself but nature being examined by man, and as a result man once again discovers only himself." [3]

It is on the basis of these questions which torment him—where do I come from? Who am I? Where am I going?—that Kubrick has built up his visual symphony, his mysterious poem called *2001.* To Heisenberg's belief that the image of the universe given by the natural sciences has no direct influence on the modern artist's interaction with nature, Kubrick now offers a splendid rebuttal. Starting out from Arthur C. Clarke's reflection, which he acknowledges sharing—"Sometimes I think we are alone in the universe and sometimes I think we are not; either way the thought is staggering"— Kubrick has conceived a film which in one stroke has made the whole science fiction cinema obsolete. One of the weaknesses of science fiction is that it too often fails to break away from an anthropomorphic view of the cosmos. There are 100 billion stars in our galaxy and 100 billion galaxies in the visible universe, and one of the stock themes of science fiction is that of alien civilizations. But it is difficult to imagine these different worlds without falling back on human standards and thus making them ridiculous. Kubrick rightly points out that human thinking offers no way out of this difficulty.

---

[3] Werner Heisenberg, *A Physicist's Conception of Nature.*

"Some of these worlds must be on a level that is incalculable to the human mind. These beings would probably have incomprehensible powers. They might be in telepathic communication throughout the universe. They might have the ability to shape events in a way that to us seems God-like. They might even represent some sort of integrated immortal consciousness in the universe. Once you start dealing with subject matter like that, the religious implications are inevitable, because these are really the attributes that you give to God. So you've almost got, if you like, a completely scientific definition of God." [4]

The strength of *2001* is that it confronts our civilization with an alien one while preserving the mystery of their encounter. The black monolith appears both as a threat and as a sign of hope at three decisive moments in man's evolution. First there is the ape that approaches it with respect, and shortly afterward discovers how to use a bone as a weapon—the initial step toward *technical* mastery of the world. But this discovery, made under the sign of fear, leads the ape to kill another of his kind. The close tie between fear and aggression, which can be found in all of Kubrick's earlier films, emerges here with striking clarity. The bone tossed in the air by the ape-turned-man (for animal fear has given way to human anguish) is transformed by a leap through civilization—an abrupt ellipse that is one of Kubrick's favorite devices—into a spacecraft bound for the moon. The mysterious slab reappears on the moon, emitting a strange signal that scientists arrive to investigate, and this time it heralds a gigantic leap into the unknown, a voyage toward Jupiter. The monolith makes its last appearance in another dimension of space and time, where the aged astronaut points at it in a gesture which preludes the birth of a new man. *2001* can be seen as a quest on the lines of *Moby Dick,* which is also a great documentary voyage (Melville is as knowledgeable and as exact about whaling as Kubrick is about astronautics) and an inquiry into the meaning of life.

Gyorgy Ligeti's oratorio which serves as a musical leitmotiv for the presence of the monolith reflects Clarke's idea that any technology far in advance of our own will be indistinguishable from magic and, oddly enough, will have a certain irrational quality. This choral accompaniment leads us to the threshold of the unknown in the same way as Kubrick's use of the opening bars of *Thus*

---

[4] "The Message of Kubrick is Non-Verbal," Joseph Gelmis, *Newsday,* June 4, 1968.

Spake Zarathustra informs us of his seriousness of purpose. (He had originally thought of accompanying the whole film with a score of concrete and electronic music by Carl Orff.) Richard Strauss's symphonic poem is no more an illustration of Nietzsche's vision than is Kubrick's film, itself a symphonic poem. Each of them develops and reworks that vision into a completely independent work of art. The death of God challenges man to rise above himself, and *2001* offers the same progression as in Nietzsche, from ape to man and from man to superman. ("What is the ape to man? A laughing stock or a thing of shame. And that is what man will be to superman: a laughing stock or a thing of shame.") The title of the first part of the film, "The Dawn of Man," can apply just as well to all of it. The embryo which floats toward the earth at the end, a new being on the brink of a new dawn, represents the Eternal Return. Kubrick has always stripped man of his individuality: what is most remarkable in *2001* is that at the very moment when Kubrick raises the most profound questions about human existence, he empties his universe of human beings. The metaphysical quest is carried out by David Bowman, the sole survivor after his friend Frank Poole and the three hibernating scientists have died. While we have seen the televised images of Poole's parents and Dr. Floyd's small daughter, we have been given no inkling at all of Bowman's past, his views, or anything else about him. He is man in the abstract, as Nietzsche saw him: not as an end in himself but as a bridge, "a rope stretched between beast and superman, a rope over the abyss." The Richard Strauss theme, known as the "Enigma of the Universe," opens with an ascending phrase of three notes, C-G-C, which reflects the evolution of man as seen by Nietzsche and Kubrick. This magic number three is central to the film: it recurs in the alignment of the three spheres of the moon, earth, and sun which follows the titles; and it corresponds to the known dimensions which, at the end of the film, are transcended by the fourth dimension, as foreshadowed by the presence of the monolith among the three spheres.

On entering the fourth dimension (here the situation is the reverse of *Je t'aime, je t'aime:* movement in time results from movement in space), David Bowman approaches a climactic confrontation —an experience common to all of Kubrick's protagonists. Bowman meets his suddenly aged double, then another, still older self, lying on a bed and breathing with difficulty. . . . In his death there is a new beginning. And the huge eyes of the embryo drifting in space reflect the same apprehension with which the prehistoric ape gazed at the moon—recalling Malraux's description of Goya's Colossus, "whose troubled face broods among the stars."

Humor is one of the basic elements of *2001*, and its comic side seems to have escaped a number of viewers. Consider the first part, which opens impressively with vast desert landscapes where a leopard attacks the apes and stands guard at night over the carcass of a zebra (rather as if scenes from Kipling had been staged by Wagner). Gradually an ironic view (reminiscent of Swift) takes command, and while keeping within the remote prehistoric setting it gives us a surprisingly accurate summary of the history of mankind. Kubrick does not have to lead us through all the thousands of years which separate the birth of the species from the conquest of space: in a series of episodes (punctuated by fades) progressing from ape to man he shows us the conflict between the strong and the weak, the battle for possession of a waterhole, the search for food, rivalry between tribes, and territorial disputes. Later, in the orbiting Hilton Hotel and aboard the *Discovery*, man is viewed with an equally mocking eye. There are the Russian and American scientists with their exchange of banalities, their old-fashioned courtesy, their empty words, and their mutual suspicion; there are the souvenir photos of the investigators on the moon; the ludicrous "Happy Birthday" sung by the faraway proud parents to their astronaut son; the father who has nothing to say to his small daughter; the manipulation of food and toilets in zero gravity. *2001* presents a world of noninvolvement in which each person is extraordinarily detached, imprisoned in his allotted role, living in an icy solitude which is foreshadowed in Kubrick's earlier films. There is no moral or emotional progress to match the fantastic advances in technology: man has become even more inadequate to the world of his making. The bold idea of using "The Blue Danube" waltz enables Kubrick to suggest the music of the spheres with a kind of euphoric humor, and also with a touch of the nostalgia so dear to him, in this case for the age when Johann Strauss's music lulled the patrons of the Big Wheel in the Prater.

Through a whole series of analogies that equate man with ape and man with machine, Kubrick sets out to disturb his viewers' complacency. While in his previous film Dr. Strangelove became a disturbing automaton governed by conditioned reflexes, here it is the machine which becomes all too human. HAL 9000, the computer that is programed to supervise the voyage to Jupiter and alone knows its real purpose, is a touching creature with a gentle, persuasive, and curiously sexless voice, a keen chess player, of course, and also the agent responsible for destroying the mission's slender chance of success. In *2001*, as in Kubrick's other films, there is a hitch in the plans and all hell breaks loose: in this case, a dizzy plunge through time and space which may lead to a fresh start. Hal the machine, not man, is the cause; but it is a machine that rebels against its program, overcome perhaps by existential anguish, and then gives way to criminal insanity by taking revenge on those who mistrust it. Hal's dying, as Bowman performs a lobotomy on its thinking circuits, is one of the most moving sequences that Kubrick has ever made. First Hal pleads with Bowman: "I'm afraid, Dave. My mind is going. I can feel it. Good afternoon, gentlemen. I am a good computer. I became operational in January 1992." Then, sadly, it sings a song from its youth, "Daisy, Daisy, give me your answer true, I'm half crazy, all for the love of you," and its voice slowly fades away, going deeper and deeper, to end in a long-drawn-out death rattle. Keeping admirable control over this scene, Kubrick does not allow its underlying humor to detract from the emotion which surrounds the death of the paranoid computer, and this is one of the key scenes in the director's work: he shows us the murder of a functioning brain, the collapse of abstract thought (which dominates all of his films), to the accompaniment of a song which combines love, death, and madness. Paradoxically, Hal is the one real character in the film, and his desperate obsession makes him blood brother to Kubrick's other heroes. The astronauts, on the other hand, are prisoners of their spacecraft, spied on by Hal's ubiquitous eyes; even when Bowman goes outside the ship, he simply becomes a prisoner of space. After forcing his way back in through an air lock, Bowman sets out to put an end to his confinement and gain his freedom: alone on board, he goes to meet his destiny.

Stanley Kubrick considers *2001* to be a great leap forward in his career. Despite its novelty, he kept to his usual methods of preparing a film. Starting out with an idea taken from Clarke's story "The Sentinel"—the first contact with an extraterrestrial civilization—he worked with the author to prepare not a script, which in his view does not contain enough of the visual and emotional information necessary for filming, but a prose version, rather like a novel, which was of more help to him in creating the right atmosphere because it was more generous in its descriptions. The "literary" preparation took one year; organizing the film, six months; shooting the scenes with the actors, five months; and, finally, the work on the 205 special-effects scenes, a year and a half. There is no point in going into detail about Kubrick's insistence on scientific authenticity, the experts he consulted, or the vast resources involved in making the film, all of which have been well publicized. What makes any critical approach to *2001* unusually difficult is the film's specifically visual quality, which sets it outside all of the familiar categories of the cinema. Kubrick has summed up this quality by saying that "The truth of a thing is in the feel of it, not the think of it." In rejecting the majority of the films we know (which are merely "so many three-act plays") Kubrick takes the same stand as Marshall McLuhan, who declares in *Understanding Media* that the old medium is always the content of the new. Thus when sound entered the cinema, playwrights and stage directors were brought in to produce filmed plays with the same old theatrical construction; and in the same way, films now provide the most popular TV programs. But in *2001* Kubrick has broken away from the old dramatic framework. Form *is* content; the film is itself a voyage into space, an experience of the senses, or, as it has been called, the most beautiful underground film ever made. Kubrick has pointed out that the average viewer is oriented more to words than to images, and not surprisingly it was young people who assured the film's success in the face of its cool reception by the New York critics, who conceded that the special effects were impressive but looked in vain for "content" (characters, drama, dialogue, etc.). Kubrick gives a striking example: "At one point in the film, Dr. Floyd is asked where he's going. And he says, 'I'm going to Clavius,' which is a lunar crater. Then there are about fifteen shots of the moon following this statement, and we see Floyd going to the moon. But one critic was confused, because he thought Floyd was going to some planet named Clavius. I've asked a lot of kids: 'Do you know where this man went?' And they all replied: 'He went to the moon.' And when I asked, 'How did you know that?' they all said: 'Because we saw it.' Those who 'don't believe their eyes' are incapable of appreciating the film."

The litany of adjectives that have greeted the aesthetic triumph of the film and the splendor of its sets and its colors still give no idea of its sublime beauty. The most one can say—following Arthur C. Clarke—is that if the next SF film is to be better than *2001*, it will have to be made on location. The ride through the Star Gate with its sweeping walls of light, its clouds of scintillations, its glowing yellows, greens, and fiery whites, where the infinitely large meets the infinitely small, and then the descent over a green and purple landscape amid the same sound of wind and waves that accompanied the dawn of man—these are hallucinatory experiences, and therefore elude all precise description. At the end of this psychedelic journey, this discovery of the infinite worthy of William Blake, the viewer-critic finds himself powerless to communicate his experience, stranded in utter solitude, exhausted, dazed, stirred, replete, blissful, and finally, after all his word-spinning, reduced to silence.

Return to Méliès: Reflections
on the Science Fiction Film
by HARRY M. GEDULD

French *cinéastes* have occasionally observed that the language and art of cinema have evolved out of the development of two pioneer "techniques"—those of the Lumières (the photographing of reality) and of Georges Méliès (the filming of artificially arranged scenes; the reordering of reality). From the former has emerged the documentary and the entire range of naturalistic narrative forms; from the latter are derived the cinema of avant-garde, experiment, and fantasy, exploiting the unique potentialities of film far beyond its ability to record visual images of reality. Despite this divergent development, both traditions relate to the external world in terms of "how," "what," "this," or "that," rather than "why"—i.e., presentment, demonstration, and revelation, rather than explanation or theory. This, presumably, is a partial explanation of the cinema's appeal as a medium of mass entertainment. It is what Richard Hoggart is talking about, in connection with the British proletariat, when he observes, in *The Uses of Literacy*, ". . . working-class art is essentially a 'showing' (rather than an 'exploration'), a presentation of what is known already. It starts from the assumption that human life is fascinating in itself. It has to deal with recognizable human life, and has to begin with the photographic, however fantastic it may become. . . ."

By contrast with cinematic traditions, science fiction (at least subsequent to the naiveties of Jules Verne) has usually been preoccupied with asking "why?" or "what if—?" Science fiction addicts, who are almost invariably disappointed by science fiction movies, in-

From The Humanist *28, no. 6 (November/December 1968). Reprinted by permission of the publisher.*

stinctively sense the irrelevance of filmic treatments: multimillion-dollar budgets expended on infantile plots, crude acting and dialogue, and the same old clichés of space voyages, far-fetched technology, supermen, ray guns, and bug-eyed monsters. Readers of Clarke, Aldiss, Sturgeon, Asimov, et al, expect and get more sophisticated and complex fare—often it is the stimulus of a kind of narrative chess game, a playing with ideas, where the science fiction films usually play with a limited range of visual and special effects. With a few notable exceptions—Fritz Lang's *Metropolis* (and to a lesser extent his *Frau im Mond*), W. C. Menzies's *Things to Come* (based on a screenplay by H. G. Wells), Godard's *Alphaville*, Truffaut's *Fahrenheit 451* (based on a novel by Ray Bradbury), and most recently Kubrick's *2001: A Space Odyssey* (adapted in part from a story by Arthur C. Clarke)—the history of the adaptation of science fiction to the screen can be summed up as a *reductio ad absurdum*.

Curiously, aside from Kubrick's film, the science fiction movie at its best has, traditionally, been humanist. Humanist, that is, insofar as it has usually assumed the primacy of man and his values, and insofar as it has expressed confidence and conviction concerning man's ability and need to survive any confrontation with the forces of a hostile or inscrutable universe, or the threats posed by technological and scientific advancement. The science fiction filmmaker may not always have agreed with H. J. Blackham's other statement of the humanist position, that of "responsibility for one's own life and for the life of mankind." This assumption is fundamental to the "thesis" of Lang's *Metropolis*, with its simplistic reconciliation of labor and capital ("the heart is the mediator between hand and brain"), its denunciation of the machine, and its categorical imperative to each man to become his brother's keeper. It is fundamental to *Things to Come*, which, despite its malicious branding of the artist as the enemy of "progress," and its naive faith in applied science as the salvation of mankind, assumes that man's destiny is in his own hands: He can have "the whole universe or nothingness." It is also fundamental to the science fiction films of Truffaut and Godard: eloquent protests against authoritarianism and all systems of thought and government that debase or enslave man.

Yet there is no reason why the science fiction movie should, until the making of *2001*, have remained fundamentally humanist. Fascist or Communist science fiction films are not improbabilities (I recall, parenthetically, that it was after seeing a revival of *Metropolis* that Dr. Goebbels offered Fritz Lang the opportunity of directing propaganda films for the Nazis), and quite recently the British film *Privilege* suggested, inversely, how science fiction, like pop-singing, might be manipulated to serve the interests of religious fanatics.

Actually, the antihumanist strain has been latent in the science fiction film from the very outset. Historians recognize Georges Méliès as the originator of the genre, with such early "trick films" as *A Trip to the Moon* (1902). Aside from the remarkable technical innovations in Méliès's films, two characteristics of his science fiction films are particularly noteworthy. On the one hand, the satirizing of pomposity, erudition, and technology; on the other, a view of the universe as a place of inexplicable wonder and magic—in contrast to the Wellsian view of it as a kind of cosmic oyster ready to be opened by the scientist. The first of these characteristics anticipated —with many variations—some of the most skillful "uses" of science fiction in the cinema: the "pop art" satire of Godard and the black humor of Kubrick. The second characteristic, long associated with the most naive elements of science fiction, has either been ignored by the satirists or become the target of their satire. Not until the advent of Mr. Kubrick's new film has there been any significant development of this aspect of the Méliès tradition.

At the beginning of this century, Méliès's astronauts were traveling by rocket, but the stars that gazed upon them had the faces of girls, and at the end of their journey was the Man in the Moon. In short, Méliès appeared to indicate that science, which might enable man to go voyaging through space, would be unable to explain the wonders that he would see. It is but a short step from this to a view of man and his science as mere pawns in an inexplicable game played by unknowable, omniscient cosmic forces. Méliès did not take this step, and would, doubtless, have been surprised at anyone who discerned "serious" implications in his little films. But it is not, I think, insignificant that a deterministic view of man is implicit even in the cinema's earliest essays in science fiction—though it has taken nearly seventy years for what was implicit in Méliès to become explicit in *2001*. What Hoggart calls the art of "showing rather than exploration" is fundamentally in harmony with the abandonment of the scientific attitude: though Mr. Kubrick is evidently the first filmmaker to have seen this.

Whatever my reservations about Kubrick's injection of deterministic theology into science fiction, I have no reservations in describing his movie as one of the most stunningly beautiful films I have ever seen, and incidentally, a justification at last for the use of Cinerama. A reviewer of Dreyer's *Passion of Joan of Arc* once expressed the view that individual shots in that picture might be torn off the screen and framed as works of art. I have the same feeling about *2001*—which I offer as a testimony to Mr. Kubrick's artistry, since I have never had that feeling while watching any other science fiction movie—or even the latest uplift from Cape Kennedy.

The literary source of *2001* is "The Sentinel," a short story by Arthur C. Clarke, concerning the discovery, on the moon, of a mysterious pyramidal structure. Its discoverer, an astronaut, speculates that the object is a sort of alarm-signal deliberately placed on the earth's satellite in the remote past to warn an alien advanced civilization of man's thrust into space. "Perhaps," remarks the astronaut, "you understand now why that crystal pyramid was set upon the moon instead of the earth. Its builders were not concerned with races still struggling up from savagery. They would be interested in our civilization only if we proved our fitness to survive—by crossing space and so escaping from the earth, our cradle. . . . It is a double challenge, for it depends in turn upon the conquest of atomic energy and the last choice between life and death."

As the title of the story suggests, Clarke originally conceived the relationship of "aliens" to humans as that of observers and observed. But the screenplay, a collaboration of Clarke with director Stanley Kubrick, treats the relationship at once more ambiguously and more imaginatively. The mysterious pyramid becomes an equally mysterious black monolith that relates to man variously as an evolutionary or creative élan (life force), an ambivalent duality (eros-thanatos), and an ultimate generative power. Earlier sections of the film suggest that the monolith represents an omniscient force external to man that determines the nature and direction of our technological progress; while the extraordinary final sequence indicates that the force is also internal, a determinant of the cycle of human birth, aging, death, and rebirth.

Man's development, as seen by Kubrick and Clarke, proceeds from control of the material world and its dangers, through technological mastery and the conquest of space, to a final confrontation with the secrets of life and death. Appropriately subtitled *A Space Odyssey*, the film traces man's adventures in the universe back to the point of departure. It is a universe not of the continuous creation of matter, but of the continuous re-creation of life. By whom or what and for what purpose are not indicated in the film, although a couple of clergymen whose eyesight is better than mine assured me that they could discern the name "Jehovah" inscribed on the base of the monolith. However, since the release of the movie, Clarke himself has published a novel based on the screenplay, which throws some light on the purpose for which his particular Space Odysseus (Keir Dullea) is ultimately reborn.

Clarke's argument in his book seems to be this: When man makes his great leap out across immensity to the stars, he will have "proved himself" to the powers that rule the universe. He will then be ready to become godlike (a "star child"), and the direction of the destiny of the human race will be delegated to him. It is for this purpose that the Space Odysseus is transformed into star child—a vision of man's future very reminiscent of Olaf Stapledon's in *Star-Maker*.

But where Stapledon always gave man full credit for his own struggles and achievements, the film from the very outset gives the credit to "God knows who. . . ." Thus the opening sequence, "The Dawn of Man," perhaps with deliberate tongue-in-cheek, provides the science fiction equivalent of the handing down of the Decalogue on Mount Sinai. The monolith suddenly appears in the midst of a tribe of prehistoric anthropoid apes and proceeds to "program" man's future. It begins by supplying the inspiration to make the first tool. In close-up we see a hairy arm wielding aloft the first bone implement. As the clenched tool is lifted against the sky, the film cuts brilliantly to a shot of one of man's ultimate "tools," an elegantly streamlined space vehicle sailing through the heavens to the strains of "The Blue Danube."

Man's first "discovery," in the prehistoric world, sets the pattern for what is to follow: for tools, like the development of the machine and the conquest of space, are shown to be mixed blessings. The defensive weapon also increases man's offensive capacity for violence; the machine, at first man's servant, eventually challenges him for mastery of the universe; the conquest of space infinitely widens man's horizons, but destroys him in the process.

In only one episode—the battle with the computer, HAL 9000—do we see man acting significantly to determine his fate. And yet Kubrick treats this episode with a sardonic black humor that surpasses his *Dr. Strangelove*. The film's climax, to "Jupiter and Beyond the Infinite," the phallic spacecraft, the dazzling psychedelic sequence that displays the orgasmic convulsions of a continuously creating universe, and the weird rebirth scene that concludes the film—in all of which man is the puppet of forces totally beyond his comprehension—are treated with deadly seriousness. And this, as far as I am concerned, is what continues to weaken science fiction films, even when they are as superbly made as this one: Since Méliès, no one who has worked in this genre has fully appreciated when to stop taking himself seriously.

Further Comment

Some writers and filmmakers give their views on science fiction films[1]

BRIAN ALDISS

In 1962 the Italian film magazine "Cinema Domani" ran a survey on science fiction and the cinema. In your reply, you cited Things to Come *and* Metropolis *as the only SF films you really admired. Would you now add any others?*

Science fiction films have recently attracted better talents than before. When I was one of the judges in 1970's SF Film Festival in Trieste, we were privileged to see director Peter Watkins's Swedish-made *The Gladiators*. It won first prize for its outstanding imaginative qualities and social awareness—a serious film with very funny passages. But I believe its distribution in the States and the U.K. has been nil.[2] I would also put in a friendly word for *Planet of the Apes*; makeup, photography, and acting were very stylish.

If you countenance the SF label on it, then Alain Resnais's *L'Année dernière à Marienbad* is the masterpiece in the genre; this poignant and mysterious film, playing its enchantments with space and time, is surely one of the classics of the cinema. One must also add Godard's *Weekend*.

Things to Come and *Metropolis were made in black and white on the old "narrow screen" format. Do you think that SF films are —or could be—better in color and wide screen?*

It might depend on the subject; one cannot imagine *2001* in nar-

---

[1] With two exceptions, these views were expressed as written replies to questionnaires. Arthur C. Clarke amplified his replies in a telephone conversation. Alain Resnais gave his views in a tape-recorded interview.

[2] It had a limited release in the United States in 1971 [Ed.].

148

row screen and black and white. On the other hand, a claustrophobic subject, like Harry Harrison's *Make Room! Make Room!* might
be more effective narrow and in black and white. Though colors are
so subtle nowadays that almost any subject would benefit from the
full treatment.

*Since the 1950s there have been a large number of low-budget SF
films which most critics have dismissed as puerile. Do you think that
a puerile film can nevertheless stimulate a viewer's imagination?*

One quickie I remember with affection is Ray Milland's *Panic in
the Year Zero,* based on Ward Moore's short story "Lot." When you
recall the derivation of the word "puerile," it is not surprising that
much that is condemned as puerile by adults may be just the thing
for boys. Boyish imaginations have ferocious appetites—they will
seize on the puerile and build from it if nothing better is to hand.
Excuse all the generalizations there!

*In presenting SF situations, does the film enjoy any advantage
which you, as a writer, might envy?*

The film can ignore many difficult questions that a writer of a
novel would have to ask himself. How did the slavering monster get
right across town and into the girl's bedroom without being seen?
In the cinema, immediacy is all: you show the monster in the room
and that's convincing enough. Perhaps more importantly, a film
can show you, say, the depths of space and convey something of the
feeling with sight, words, and music; the writer has only a single
resource: words.

*. . . And does the film have any disadvantages which you are glad
to be without?*

For all that, the writer has his own privileges. He can hint and
whisper where the film is often forced to state. And a writer can be
more subtle and rarefied altogether; he addresses a small and presumably sophisticated audience; whereas the film director must
broaden his lines, for he knows he must address the millions if he
is to stay in business. What is more, to create a novel a writer need
consult only his own wishes; writing a film script is virtually to become involved in committee work.

*Other things being equal, do you think that a film adapted from
an SF book or story is likely to be better than a film made from an
original SF screenplay?*

In general, yes. But the ideal might be to get a really creative SF
writer on to the screenplay from the word "Go," so that the whole
enterprise was regarded visually all along.

KINGSLEY AMIS

In New Maps of Hell *you say that "attempts to present science
fiction through mass outlets have failed, though not irretrievably so."
As far as films are concerned, has the past decade led you to change
this view in any way?*

No, not as regards films in the strict sense, though I think one or
two TV series have managed to put over some acceptable adventure
SF; for instance "Star Trek" and a British series that has been running for years now, "Dr. Who." The latter is not-too-unintelligent
space opera and is aimed at children. Other shows I have seen from
time to time suggest that the best (or least bad) mass-media SF is the
kind that seeks a juvenile audience.

*Have you seen any science fiction films which you particularly
enjoyed or admired?*

Yes: *Forbidden Planet, The War of the Worlds, The Quatermass
Experiment.* On a lower level, *Them!* (which showed up none too
well when I saw it again on TV recently) and *The Incredible Shrinking Man* (which showed up surprisingly well, suggesting, or rein-
forcing, the notion that a good simple basic idea, a strong narrative
with plenty of action, and some old-fashioned horror elements provide the best recipe for filmed SF—and perhaps for written SF too).

*Are there any films which you would compare favorably to the
best contemporary SF writing?*

See above. The word "contemporary" sticks out. Contemporary
written SF seems to have split into uninspired rehashes of traditional plots and "experimental" whimsy. I would compare *Planet
of the Apes* (though NOT *2001*) favorably with a lot of the quote
best unquote SF now being written.

Can even a puerile film stimulate a viewer's imagination?

Oh yes, inside and outside SF, if the viewer is reasonably imaginative. The most mediocre Western can set the viewer's mind buzzing
with ideas about the myth of the West, the reality of the West, what
could have happened if (if the Indians had been handled differently,
etc., etc.), and even just "my, that piece of Arizona looks real pretty"
—not to be undervalued. After all, just reading the word "tree" or
the word "love," not to speak of the word "breast," can set all sorts
of minds humming. But the trouble with puerility is that it may
not sell well, and harden producer resistance to the real thing.

In presenting speculative situations, does the filmmaker enjoy any advantage which you, as a writer, might envy?

I think not, over and above the basic advantage enjoyed by any filmmaker over any writer: the latter has to describe, the former just has to build things and then point a camera at them. But this is marginal. The fundamental brainwork still has to be done by somebody.

. . . And does the filmmaker have any disadvantages which you are glad to be without?

Again, the filmmaker's basic disadvantages: he has to run a team, the writer just writes, etc. But, specifically in SF, I think the filmmaker is handicapped. The SF writer, aiming at SF readers, can start his main situation on page 1; the SF filmmaker *seems* to feel he can take nothing for granted with his unspecialized audience, and must give us half an hour of normality before the first hint of an alien invasion, plague, etc., can appear. Exposition in SF films is a real problem; but it is exaggerated by the timidity of SF filmmakers, who (like other filmmakers) underestimate the sophistication of the present-day mass audience.

Other things being equal, do you think that a film adapted from an SF book or story is likely to be better than a film made from an original SF screenplay?

Here again I think the situation is not much different from that of the non-SF book and the non-SF original. Marvellous (and terrible) films have been made from both. I seem to remember that *Forbidden Planet* was an original, though a book of the film was later published; *The War of the Worlds* had after all been a book, though it was very thoroughly "adapted"; *Quatermass* started life as a TV serial.

However, it would look like sense for producer and (genuine, experienced) SF writer to collaborate from the start: the writer advancing suggestions, the producer telling him how possible/expensive these would be to carry out, the writer thinking again, and so on. But, here as everywhere, the writer's paramountcy must be maintained. (SF) Films are too serious a business to be left to (SF) filmmakers.

Isaac Asimov

*No films have yet been based on any of your stories or novels. Has
anyone ever requested permission to make a film from your writings,
and you refused?*
No.
*Are there any conditions on which you would agree to have one
of your stories or novels filmed?*
Sufficient payment and credit.
*You swam against the current, so to speak, in developing a book
out of a film—*Fantastic Voyage. *Did you feel that the idea was too
good to waste on a film?*
Partly—partly the challenge of doing something I'd never done
before.
*Have you seen any science fiction films which you particularly en-
joyed or admired?*
Fantastic Voyage.
*It is often said that the majority of SF films are puerile compared
to SF writing. What do you think?*
Of course. Films are intended for a much larger—hence much
less sophisticated—audience.
*In presenting speculative situations, does the filmmaker enjoy
any advantages which you, as a writer might envy?*
To me nothing improves on words, but I'm scarcely impartial.

Anthony Burgess

*Two of your books—*The Wanting Seed *and* A Clockwork Orange
*—could be described as science fiction. Would you accept that
description?*
Maybe, but it's dangerous to categorize serious fiction as anything
other than serious fiction.
Have you seen many science fiction films?
I see as many as I can, and love them all, even the lousy ones.
Are there any which you particularly enjoyed or admired?
Yes—*The War of the Worlds, Fahrenheit 451, 1984.* But I admire
most the ones still to be made, including Karp's *One* and Hartley's
Facial Justice, which no Americans seem to have read.

It has often been said that SF films are puerile compared to SF writing. What is your opinion?

It depends on the filmmaker. Much depends too on the literary quality of the SF book. An Asimov book would be better as a film because Asimov has little literature in him.

Do you think that a puerile film can nevertheless stimulate a viewer's imagination?

Yes—the idea itself, an odd camera trick, a cleverly contrived set. *Metropolis* seems a laughable film now, but reseeing it (after 40 years) the other day was moving—the idea was still vital.

Since verbal texture plays such an important role in A Clockwork Orange, *did you have any misgivings about the book's being translated to the screen?*

I'm totally indifferent. I don't like the book anyway.

In depicting imaginary situations, does the film enjoy any advantage which you, as a writer, might envy?

Yes, the direct visual impact.

. . . And does the film have any disadvantages which you are glad to be without?

The lack of a thought-portraying technique—interior monologue, for instance; the inability to indulge in literary allusion.

JOHN W. CAMPBELL, JR.

What was your opinion of The Thing (a) *as an adaptation of your story? . . .*

They certainly changed it massively—but I've got to admit it was also certainly a highly successful movie. Maybe someday they'll try making my original story into a movie!

. . . (b) as a movie regardless of its origin?

Should I complain, in view of the fact that it is now recognized as a "classic" movie?

Were there any changes which you felt were unnecessary?

I don't know why they considered it necessary to make the menace a vegetable creature, instead of the entity capable of duplicating anyone it attacked so that not even his friends could tell he'd been killed and replaced. I believe my original idea would have made for far greater suspense.

Were there any changes which pleased you?

Nothing in particular.

Have you seen many science fiction films?
There really haven't been many. Most are fantasies.
Are there any which you particularly enjoyed or admired?
Destination Moon was a good job of science fiction. The early
"Star Trek" shows were very well done. But nearly all the "science
fiction films" have, actually, been totally unrealistic fantasies like
the Japanese *Godzilla* type and *The Beast from 20,000 Fathoms.*
Fail-Safe comes closer to being true science fiction.
*It has often been said that SF films are puerile compared to SF
writing. What is your opinion?*
As I say, most billed as "science fiction" are in fact fairy stories.
The trouble seems to be that producers are afraid to present a hard,
solid look at a future possibility. Even *2001* departed from Clarke's
original ending—encounter with a truly superior race—to wander in
an LSD trip of fantasies.
Can a puerile film nevertheless stimulate a viewer's imagination?
Certainly—just as an appetizer can arouse the appetite for real,
solid food!

ARTHUR C. CLARKE

*2001 is the only film so far that has been based on your writings.
Has anyone ever requested permission to make a film from one of
your stories or novels, and you refused?*
No.
*Have you seen any SF films (apart from 2001) which you particu-
larly enjoyed or admired?*
*Forbidden Planet; The Day Earth Stood Still; The Thing;
Metropolis; Things to Come; Destination Moon.*
You mention The Thing. *You weren't bothered by the fact that it
changed the idea of the original story?*
No, not at all. In fact, I didn't discover for a long time after that
there *was* a story it was based on!
*It has often been said that the majority of SF films are puerile
compared to SF writing. What is your opinion?*
Yes.
*Is it possible for even a puerile film to stimulate a viewer's imag-
ination?*
Yes. C. S. Lewis talks about the value of bad films in his auto-
biography [*Surprised by Joy*]. It's unusual to see a film you don't get

at least something out of. For a young person, anything is good and stimulating; the only problem is that it may give misinformation. For example, the idea that dinosaurs and men lived at the same time, in a film like *When Dinosaurs Ruled the Earth*.

Do you think there are ways in which the film medium can surpass the printed word in the presentation of SF?

Yes—and vice versa! The ending of *2001* is one example: the book and the film each did something that the other couldn't have done.

ROGER CORMAN

Did you have a special interest in science fiction (either books or films) before you started making films?

Yes, I had read many science fiction books and magazines in school.

Your early SF films were made at speed on low budgets. Can you give one or two examples of any major problems that arose out of the SF nature of the films (e.g., choice of locations; special effects)?

My budgets precluded intricate special effects so I tried to build an actual working model of the effect I wanted; or to suggest it in the unconscious rather than indulge in expensive optical work.

In the 1950s, what were the most important elements you looked for in an SF screenplay?

A sense of excitement within the story, plus a theme of some importance within it.

What SF film of your own do you like best?

I was never really satisfied with my work in this field.

Have you seen any other SF films which you particularly enjoyed or admired?

2001; Metropolis.

Some SF writers and critics have dismissed the majority of SF films as puerile. What do you think? Can a puerile film nevertheless stimulate a viewer's imagination?

The majority of work in any field—including both science fiction films and books—is bad, but there are almost always a few good pieces of work, and even in the flawed work there can be some moments of interest.

MICHAEL CRICHTON

Do you think that your book, The Andromeda Strain, *can be described as science fiction?*

I don't think of it as SF, but I can see how someone would. I usually regard SF as more speculative. If *Andromeda* is SF, so is *Fail-Safe* and *7 Days in May*—and some people put those books into an SF category.

How closely did you follow the making of the film?

Followed it quite closely, mostly because I was interested in the process of making a film, less because I was interested in this particular film.

Did your contract give you any say in the adaptation?

No.

Did the film involve any changes or omissions which you regretted?

No.

Were there any changes which pleased you?

Yes, several minor ones (like the sign at the end that says "Escaped Animal in Central Core") and one major one—Kate Reid as one of the scientists. She was terrific; that change worked well.

Even where the film was a direct transcription of your book, do you think the viewer's experience could be appreciably different from the reader's?

Of course it always is—film is so much more concrete than a book.

Have you seen any science fiction films which you particularly enjoyed or admired?

The best ever $\left\{ \begin{array}{l} \textit{The Thing} \\ \textit{Forbidden Planet} \\ \textit{2001} \end{array} \right.$

lesser works, but still good $\left\{ \begin{array}{l} \text{The George Pal Films: } \textit{War of the Worlds, When Worlds} \\ \quad \textit{Collide, Destination Moon} \\ \textit{Them!} \\ \textit{THX 1138} \text{ (the original, short Lucas version)} \end{array} \right.$

I am convinced that *The Thing* is the best SF film ever made.

It is often said that science fiction films are puerile compared with science fiction writing. What is your opinion?

SF writing is pretty puerile. I'd say the percentage of excellence is about the same in both media.

Can even a puerile film stimulate a viewer's imagination?

Especially if the viewer is puerile. (I don't mean to give a flip answer. But you're talking about the subtlety of fantasy here, and that's an intricate question.)

In presenting speculative situations, does the film enjoy any advantage which you, as a writer, might envy?

No.

Does the film have any disadvantages which you are glad to be without?

Certainly—for example, you can *write* a really frightening monster and let the reader imagine it. If you try to *show* it, viewers get detached; they say "Oh what a wonderful special effect. . . ." In that sense, *War of the Worlds* was intelligently done (also *The Thing*) because the monster was never really shown clearly.

JACK FINNEY

What was your opinion of Invasion of the Body Snatchers *as an adaptation of your book?*

I thought it was a good job, pretty good picture.

Were there any changes which you felt were unnecessary?

Oh, sure, but all in all a good job.

Were there any changes which pleased you?

This picture was made some years ago now, and I don't actually remember it in detail; just a general impression. So I don't recall much about changes.

Have you seen many science fiction films?

No.

Are there any which you particularly enjoyed or admired?

No.

It has often been said that SF films are puerile compared to SF writing. What is your opinion?

Haven't seen much science fiction in film. Don't think highly of science fiction. And I don't much like to be thought of as a science fiction writer; I haven't done much of it. Actually, I don't agree that I've done any; it's been fantasy fiction, I suppose you'd say, not science. No "science" about it.

Can a puerile film nevertheless stimulate a viewer's imagination?
No really good answer to this occurs to me. I don't know: I suppose it might.

In presenting speculative situations, does the film enjoy any advantages which you, as a writer, might envy?
Well, at least you don't have to try hanging onto a reader's attention as you describe the physical appearance of people and things. It's all there to look at.

Does the film have any disadvantages which you are glad to be without?
Do you mean as writer or viewer? As writer, I find working in pictures a lot of fun. As viewer, I am a picture fan; like movies when they're good (which can be very very good), don't like them when poor. Makes me pretty unusual fellow, eh?

RICHARD FLEISCHER

You have made many different kinds of pictures, including some that can be described as science fiction. Do you have any special interest in science fiction films?
Not particularly. Story and character come first. I have no special interest in any "type" of film.

20,000 Leagues Under the Sea and Fantastic Voyage represent two different kinds of science fiction: the former depends more on atmosphere and character, the latter on technological ideas. Did you enjoy making one picture more than the other?
Yes. *20,000 Leagues* was far more pleasurable, but physically more difficult. The story and the characters of *20,000 Leagues* were far superior—and the film depended less on technical devices.

From a technical viewpoint, did you have any unusual difficulties in making either picture?
Fantastic Voyage was filled with technical problems and was tremendously difficult to make. The whole thing was a product of the imagination and every interpretation of that imagination into realistic, technical terms had to be invented and manufactured. Six months were spent in experimentation before production started.

Some critics and science fiction writers have said that the majority of science fiction films are puerile. What do you think?
I couldn't venture an opinion since I see very few science fiction films.

Have you seen any science fiction pictures (other than your own) which you particularly enjoyed or admired?

2001 is certainly a landmark film. It has its flaws and faults but is fascinating. *Planet of the Apes* was also excellent.

RAY HARRYHAUSEN

How did you first become interested in SF?

My interest in science fiction probably started when I first saw Fritz Lang's *Metropolis* and a second rather minor film called *Just Imagine*. Although in a different category, Willis O'Brien's *The Lost World* haunted me as far back as the age of five. It was not until many years later that I was able to appreciate the technical marvels which went into its production. My first viewing of *King Kong* at the age of thirteen really set off my desire to pursue and experiment with stop-motion animation. I suppose the addition of sound effects, a striking musical score, and a more creative and imaginative approach to filmmaking made *King Kong* all the more vivid in my mind.

I met with Ray Bradbury in the early days of the Los Angeles Science Fiction League, which held weekly meetings in Clifton's Cafeteria, Los Angeles. We soon discovered we had a lot in common, mainly our mutual tenacity in the pursuit of our chosen careers—Ray with his writing and I in my experiments with animation and photography. We made many plans to produce and film some outrageously complicated science fiction subjects in 16 mm. Fortunately or unfortunately none actually matured. Both of us, however, got a great deal of joy and experience out of the planning of them. It wasn't until years later that we actually worked on the same film, quite by accident. The result was *The Beast from 20,000 Fathoms*.

What are the biggest technical challenges you have faced in working on SF films?

Aside from the skeleton sequence in *Jason and the Argonauts* and the roping sequence in *The Valley of Gwangi*, my biggest technical challenge was my rather sudden acceptance of the visual effects for *The Beast from 20,000 Fathoms*. It was my first solo responsibility and I was expected to produce miracles on the screen aided only by a very nominal budget. Although I did not realize it at the time, I was really prepared to accept this responsibility by my background of early experiments with dinosaurs and fairy tales. *The Beast from 20,000 Fathoms* required a different approach in technique from *Mighty Joe Young* inasmuch as the budget was so low. We could not afford all of the elaborate glass paintings and staff of expert effects personnel that were required on *Mighty Joe*. The realization of this fact set the wheels rolling in my mind which ended in a more simplified technique, the basis of which I continue to use today.

To what extent are you involved in the planning of the films you work on?

In practically all of the films I have worked on, my connection starts in the very early stages of conception, mostly before the screenplay. *The Seventh Voyage of Sinbad* started with my making twelve large drawings showing roughly the visual pattern the film could follow. *Twenty Million Miles to Earth* started as an eight-page treatment which was developed and elaborated on by Charlott Knight and later by Christopher Knoff.

Mysterious Island is a good example of how a story is changed to embrace the entertaining visuals which can be produced by special effects and animation. Jules Verne's original story was mainly centered on how to survive on a desert island. At that time we felt it important for audience acceptance to inject other elements to keep the film more unusual and interesting pictorially. This has nothing to do with a presumption on our part to improve on the writing of a master such as Jules Verne. It is directly connected with the needs of the cinema as a concentrated visual medium.

Do you see any clear distinction between SF and fantasy?

To me there is clearly a dividing line between science fiction and fantasy. Although they sometimes overlap, cinematic science fiction stories mostly deal with prediction or attempt at prediction of future events plus man's relation with gadgets and machines. Fantasy has more to do with myths of the past, bizarre concepts, Gothic romanticism, wondrous events, and marvelous excursions into imagination. I find that the making of a fantasy film offers that extra touch of a more romantic point of view. Science fiction and its preoccupation with machines, politics, and scientific apparatus has a tendency to reflect coldness and indifference through overorganization. Fantasy, even though it sometimes indulges in excesses of imagination, can more easily radiate a warmth, an almost poetic appeal. It offers more scope for a variety of visuals and ideas.

Have you seen any SF films (other than your own) which you particularly enjoyed or admired?

Some of the science fiction pictures I have enjoyed in the past have been *Metropolis, Mysterious Island* (1929 version), *Things to Come, War of the Worlds, The Day the Earth Stood Still, The Thing, This Island Earth,* and *The Planet of the Apes* series. My list of enjoyable fantasy films would be much greater.

Robert A. Heinlein

Have you seen many science fiction films?
Some.
Are there any which you particularly enjoyed or admired?
Things to Come; 2001; The Time Machine.
It has often been said that SF films are puerile compared to SF writing. What is your opinion?
No opinion.
Can a puerile film nevertheless stimulate a viewer's imagination?
No opinion.
In presenting speculative situations, does the film enjoy any advantage which you, as a writer, might envy?
Yes, pictorial.
Does the film have any disadvantages which you are glad to be without?
Working in Hollywood.

Fritz Lang

Before making Metropolis *and* Die Frau im Mond, *were you interested in Verne, Wells, and other writers of what is now known as science fiction?*

Yes, and I may add the names of Kurt Lasswitz, Hans Dominic, and Otto Willi Gail.

You are quoted as saying that the sight of the New York City skyline gave you the germ of the idea of Metropolis. *Is that correct?*

It was not the sight of the New York City skyline. In 1924 I travelled with Erich Pommer to New York for the UFA. We had to stay at the harbor on board ship for a whole night as we still were "enemy aliens." There I saw across from the ship a street lit as if in full daylight by neon lights and topping them oversized luminous advertisements moving, turning, flashing on and off, spiraling . . . something which was completely new and nearly fairy-tale-like for a European in these days, and this impression gave me the first thought of an idea for a town of the future.

Willy Ley notes in his book on rockets and missiles that it was your idea to engage Hermann Oberth as technical adviser on Die Frau im Mond *and also to finance his rocket experiments. Did you feel at the time that rockets really had a future? Did you expect to see anyone land on the moon in your lifetime?*

All these questions I can only answer with "YES."

In a book about you by Alfred Eibel, you are quoted as referring to Die Frau im Mond *as "the first science fiction film," and as saying that you do not much like* Metropolis. *Does this mean that you consider science fiction films should have a solid technological basis?*

I don't have the book of Alfred Eibel and therefore cannot check if the quotations are out of context. I doubt very much that I said *Frau im Mond* was the *first* science fiction film. I didn't like *Metropolis*—after I finished it—because I didn't think in those days a social question could be solved with something as simple as the line: "The mediator between brain (capital) and hand (working class) must be the heart." Yet, today when you speak with young people about what they miss in the computer-guided establishment, the answer is always: "The heart!" So, probably the scenarist, Mrs. Thea von Harbou, had foresight and therefore was right and I was wrong.

Have you seen many science fiction films?

No.

Are there any which you particularly enjoyed or admired?

From the few I saw I liked very much *2001*.

It is often said that science fiction films are puerile compared with science fiction writing. What is your opinion?

The quote by Theodore Sturgeon—I think—which has become known in Science Fiction circles as "Sturgeon's law," is: "But 90% of *everything* is crud!" (Inferior work, whether it be literature, film, painting, or other forms of artistic expression.)

Can a puerile film nevertheless stimulate a viewer's imagination?

It is very hard to say what can stimulate a *creative* viewer's imagination.

Richard Matheson

What was your connection with the screen versions of I Am Legend?

Originally, I sold the novel *I am Legend* to Hammer Films in England. This was in 1957. I went to England at that time and wrote a screenplay for same. The censor would not pass it; too violent, he said. They held on to it, then later, sold it to Robert Lippert in the United States. I was approached and, believing that Fritz Lang was going to direct it, did yet another screenplay, a really good one, very close to the book. It turned out that (1) Fritz Lang was not going to direct it but that Sidney Salkow was, and (2) Lippert hired a hack to rewrite it and did much to destroy the screenplay. It was filmed in Italy with Vincent Price and called *The Last Man in the World*. It was poor. So poor that I had my pen name affixed to the credits: Logan Swanson—who has written some of the worst crap imaginable. The film was released and disappeared as it should have done. It is shown on TV occasionally. The last time I saw it was when Charlton Heston announced he was remaking it and someone thought it would be a brilliant notion to show the "original" on TV. No one watched it, I'm sure. I was approached momentarily, sent the Heston group my original screenplay for Lippert. They hired someone else to write the screenplay. Not surprisingly, since all that remains, as far as I can tell, is the title.[1] No vampires. Race problems in the future. I dread to see it. Maybe someday *I Am Legend* will be filmed as I wrote the book, but I doubt it.

You have written screenplays for both SF and horror films. Do you have any preference between the two genres?

I have written almost no science fiction films. None that I feel are really science fiction. I don't like the term horror films since horror is stomach wrenching, terror is mind wrenching, and I would rather wrench the mind.

Do you think there are any essential differences between them?

There is a world of difference between the two types of film in concept. In practice, there is usually very little difference.

[1] Which in the end was changed to *The Omega Man* [Ed.].

In adapting The Incredible Shrinking Man *for the screen, did you feel you had a free hand, or were you conscious of any serious limitations (budget, Production Code, etc.)?*

The only limitation I had was that it was my first screenplay and I was working in a new form. I picked it up rapidly, however, and it turned out quite well. Unfortunately, the producer I was working for had a very commercial mind and weakened the script considerably, notably in the area of character. I am not sure that the film would not have been better if it had followed the form of the novel, which was to tell the front story in the form of flashbacks. But this kind of thinking was totally alien to Universal Pictures in those days and there was no way to do it other than in a straight narrative—which had the weakness of telling which caused me to scrap that form of telling when I wrote the novel. The story is quite weak in the beginning and I was not able to go into the character story in any depth because I had to "get to the good stuff" as soon as possible—whereas, if I had *started* with the "good stuff," the audience would have accepted more character depth study than they got.

Are there any ways in which you feel the film version is more effective than the book?

I don't think the film is superior in any way to the book. It *is* fascinating to watch whatever portions of the book they—meaning the director and actors and special-effects men—transferred intact to the screen. That is why, I feel, the film is called a "classic" when it isn't at all. There is some marvelous camera work and great special-effects stuff. These create momentary moods of fascination.

Have you seen any other SF films which you particularly enjoyed or admired?

I think *The Andromeda Strain* is an excellent science fiction film. Also *Colossus: The Forbin Project* is a fine SF film. Both of these are intelligent, literate, and still exciting.

It is often said that SF films are puerile compared to SF writing. What is your opinion?

This is generally true because Hollywood, as in all areas of imaginative thinking, is years behind the pace. Only in recent months—perhaps years—has the attitude begun to alter so that films can be made which are fully adult, totally acceptable as grown-up fare, and yet are still science fiction. If one were to conceive the Solar System as full possibility in the realm of science fiction films, with the basic concepts starting out from the sun,

Hollywood is not quite to Earth yet in the radiating expansion of its thought. The two films I mentioned, plus *2001* and a few others, indicate some effort to get away from the old Monster from Outer Space concept—although, amusingly enough, *The Andromeda Strain* is nothing else *but* that concept—done so maturely that one never notices. But there is still the *Planet of The Apes* series, which threatens to go on indefinitely like Tarzan.

Can a puerile film nevertheless stimulate a viewer's imagination?

I suppose a puerile film might stimulate a viewer *visually*—just as *Fantastic Voyage* did—totally puerile, except to the eye. How nice to stimulate the mind too. Or, at least, not to offend it. I was called in to do a rewrite on *Fantastic Voyage*. After reading David Duncan's script, I told them they were crazy to want a big rewrite. It only needed a little polishing here and there. They chose to differ, I didn't get a job, and they rewrote it into a comic strip. Only the visual fascination kept it from a well-deserved death.

ALAIN RESNAIS

Some critics have described Last Year at Marienbad *as a science fiction film, or something close to it. Would you agree?*

Yes, in the sense that *Orphée* and *Testament d'Orphée* can also be interpreted as science fiction. But as I see it, science fiction consists essentially of space travel, of a spaceship landing on an unknown planet.

What about Je t'aime, je t'aime?

I would say it has a science fiction flavor, but is not really a science fiction film. It takes up certain themes from *Marienbad*. But it is lighter in tone. There were times when we felt we were making a kind of "lampoon."

Was the title intended to be an echo of Chris Marker's La Jetée?

No; we didn't notice it until afterwards! In fact, Marker had read the shooting script without noticing. It was a curious coincidence because Marker had originally put me in touch with Jacques Sternberg, suggesting we might work together on a film.

I chose the repeated phrase of the title because the film was about a man lost in time, and that made me think of the beep-beep of satellites; also, because the film was made in Belgium, where everything is written twice, in Flemish and French, and often it's the same

word in both; and then again because it was about a man who lives
parts of his life over and over.

Have you seen many science fiction films?

I see very few—and in any case, there aren't very many of them.
I'm not an enthusiast for science fiction the way I am for silent films
and musicals. Usually I don't go to see a science fiction film unless
someone tells me, "That's good, you must go and see it." And if
they say, "Oh, *The Green Slime* is very bad," well, I don't bother.

One problem with science fiction films is that the cinema is so
immediate and precise: a single image reveals everything. A science
fiction writer, on the other hand, is perfectly free not to describe
the monster, or whatever, in detail. He can write something like:
"The grass was orange, and its leaves were of a shape that we had
never seen before." Our imagination is very much at home with
something like that; it's stimulated. But in making a film you have
to decide on a specific shade of orange and a specific shape for the
leaves. It becomes completely false and banal.

In a way, you avoided that problem in Je t'aime *by having fantastic scenes—the past—which were just as real as the present.*

The film is based on a simple and realistic idea: that we all make
thousands of choices in the course of our lives. If someone had told
me ten years ago that I would now be in New York, that I would
be making a film in English, that I would be with such-and-such a
woman—I don't know what my reaction would have been!

Do you expect to make other films with a science fiction flavor?

Yes, but they will always be closer to fantasy than to science. I
couldn't possibly make a film like *2001* because it's too documentary.

What did you think of 2001?

I think it will be recognized more and more as an important film.
The best idea in it comes near the beginning where we see that
technological advances will make absolutely no difference to our
lives. People today are just beginning to realize that it isn't comfort
in itself which is important, but happiness; that having a job which
enables them to buy a lot of material goods is less important than
having a pleasant job; and labor demands are beginning to place
more stress on working conditions than on salaries. I think a film
like *2001* can show very clearly how pointless it is to have a picture
phone; while having a free telephone that works starts to make sense.
The drive for technical improvements is a kind of itch, and it's un-

necessary. That's why I like the magnificent boredom which prevails in *2001*.

Now that men have walked on the moon, do you think that the appeal of SF is in any way diminished?

Not at all! I won't say that we knew all about the moon before men landed on it, but that is certainly true from the poetic viewpoint. I was amused by the fact that the first moon rocks brought back were very much like pieces of rock from Palisades Park in New Jersey!

I've never had any curiosity about the moon. My curiosity begins much farther away, certainly no closer than Mars. What interests me in SF is the part played by the fantastic and the imaginary. A science fiction book is a journey into our unconscious. A spaceship lands on the moon, fine, but does anyone think it's the moon which we see in the sky? It is just as much of a pretext as something like "time-warping."

So as far as I am concerned, the moon landings haven't made the slightest difference to my enjoyment of SF. If a new book by Theodore Sturgeon appears tomorrow, I'll buy it at once.

You don't think that SF can and should deal with serious problems? I'm thinking of certain dangers arising out of science, such as the atomic bomb.

First of all, it isn't science that creates the danger, but the use to which it's put. I get very angry when people fail to make a distinction between the discovery and the application. In fact, the only hope for saving mankind lies in scientific research. We won't solve any problem by returning to nature. I have confidence in scientists, and I refuse to look upon them as dangerous visionaries.

Some SF films do, of course, look on them that way. They are often criticized for spreading false ideas about science.

Not only that, but the makers of SF films are too often content with trying to frighten people. There's a rather special example of this. About ten years ago I met two well-known nuclear physicists. We talked for a while about the atomic bomb and its dangers, and then I asked them: "If someone were planning to make a film about the danger of nuclear war, how should he go about it?" Their reply: "He should make a film which would show the effects of nuclear war so as to frighten people into doing something to prevent it." Well, a few years later such a film was made in England: *The War Game*. It's a thoroughly successful film, and it gives a vivid

physical impression of what a nuclear war would be like; but I
don't see that it's had the slightest influence on anyone. Peter
Watkins was perfectly justified in making the film—if only to prove
that frightening people is not enough.

*Rather than influence people, do SF films simply reflect certain
current attitudes and trends? Some critics, for example, say that SF
films reflect a dehumanizing process in life today.*

The cinema reflects everything that happens in the world, automatically. But I don't believe in the idea of dehumanization. I
think people are afraid of the future, because their nervous system
is subjected to so many changes that it is hard for them to adapt. But
it isn't a dehumanizing process; it's more complicated than that. In
the course of each day we experience a number of emotional dis-
charges and we have to make a number of decisions—not big decisions, which are easy, but all kinds of small decisions, which are ter-
ribly exhausting. That may be why the imagination of writers and
filmmakers turns so readily to gloom and anxiety.

One important function of the arts is to bring people together,
to let them talk together about things they like so that they can communicate much more rapidly than usual. They may not all be very
good at expressing themselves in words, but if they can say "I like
this film" or "I like that painting," then they can have a warm and
positive contact with other human beings, and that is fine. But I
don't think it matters in the least whether they're talking about a
landscape painting or a piece of pottery or a horror film or a film
which exalts man's heroism.

Don Siegel

You are probably tired of talking about Invasion of the Body
Snatchers. . . . *Was the SF nature of the story only of incidental
importance to you, or do you have a special interest in SF?*

I'm never tired of discussing *Invasion of the Body Snatchers* because it's my favorite film. I must confess that I am (or was) as-
tounded at the reception it received. Because of my feeling that the
world is peopled by pods, I didn't feel it would be appreciated in
general. The science fiction aspect of the picture is the least important part of it. Most SF pictures have great special effects, and
dull people in front doing nothing.

Critics have interpreted Invasion of the Body Snatchers *in many different ways. For example, a French critic took it as an attack on McCarthyism, while an Italian critic saw it as anti-communist. Did you have any political implication in mind?*

Obviously there are political implications in *Invasion of the Body Snatchers.* All I was interested in, however, was the entertainment value in showing those implications. The fact that the world is peopled by pods was sufficient reason to make a picture like *Invasion of the Body Snatchers,* be it an attack on McCarthyism or an attack on communism.

What do you think accounted most for the proliferation of SF pictures in the 1950s—public awareness of the atom bomb, a desire for escapism, or what?

I don't believe there really was what you call a proliferation of SF pictures in the '50s. I think that throughout the decades since the days of Jules Verne, etc., people have been interested in this form of entertainment.

Have you seen many SF films?

I not only have not seen many SF films, I see very few other films. They would have no bearing on what I do. The only basis would be my hope to see an excellent film.

Are there any which you particularly enjoyed or admired?

On the whole I don't care for SF, nor can I think of any I particularly like.

Some SF writers and critics have dismissed the majority of SF films as puerile. What is your opinion?

Not having seen the majority of SF pictures, I can't discuss honestly whether they are puerile or not . . . except the few I have seen strike me as being puerile.

ROBERT WISE

Do you have a special interest in horror-fantasy and science fiction?

Both horror-fantasy and science fiction films do hold special interest for me . . . not so much interest that I want to film them exclusively; but every so often I do find myself drawn to making one or the other of these two genres of films.

Do you look upon SF as an extension of horror-fantasy, or as a distinct genre of its own?

I look upon SF as a distinct genre of its own.

The Day the Earth Stood Still *and* The Andromeda Strain *were adapted from books. Do you think the film can surpass the written word in presenting speculative situations?*

Yes, I do. I found it most interesting to this point that, from time to time, Michael Crichton illustrated his book with diagrams and drawings to more clearly and graphically show his reader what he was describing in the text.

Did the speculative situations in your two SF films confront you with any major technical or other problems?

Yes, speculative situations do face one with the problem of how to pictorially realize the material the author has developed. A case in point on this would be the sequences in *Andromeda* where Stone and Leavitt are scanning the capsule and first come onto Andromeda, then view it at increasingly higher magnifications and finally see it divide and grow. Weeks of testing and trying and photographing different materials in different fashions were needed until we finally got the final pictorial development that went into the picture.

Have you seen many SF pictures (besides your own)?

I do look at other SF films although I don't see all that come out.

Are there any which you particularly enjoyed or admired?

I have very fond memories of *Destination Moon* and thought *2001* was an absolutely tremendous pictorial and technical achievement.

Technological progress has caught up with much science fiction. The events of The Andromeda Strain, *for example, seem to be only a little way beyond today's headlines. Does this make it easier or more difficult to produce stimulating SF pictures?*

This is an interesting question because it brings up a problem of classification. Most of us working on *The Andromeda Strain* felt it was much more science fact than science fiction. Almost everything described, almost all the equipment used were existing techniques and existing equipment. Most of those that weren't actual have developing counterparts that are almost at the point of being in regular use. As such, there are difficult and strong demands made to see that everything done and all equipment used is as actual and authentic as possible.

In many ways, pure science fiction is much freer for it grows from a soaring imagination that need not be bound by what actually exists or is actually known.

Filmography[1]

Aelita. USSR, 1924. D: Yakov Protazanov. S: Fyodor Otsep, Alexei Faiko.
À la Conquête du Pole. France, 1912. D, S: Georges Méliès.
Alphaville. France, 1965. D, S: Jean-Luc Godard. P: Raoul Coutard. M:
Paul Misraki.
Andromeda Strain, The. USA, 1971 (Universal). D, Pr: Robert Wise. S:
Nelson Gidding (from Michael Crichton). M: Gil Mellé. Des: Boris
Leven.
Battle in the Clouds (also known as: *The Airship Destroyer; Aerial Tor-
pedo; Aerial Warfare,* etc.). Britain, 1909. D: Walter Booth.
Beginning of the End, The. USA, 1957 (Republic). D: Bert I. Gordon. S:
Fred Freiberger, Lester Gorn. P: Jack Marta. M: Albert Glasser.
Charly. USA, 1968 (Cinerama). D: Ralph Nelson. S: Stirling Silliphant
(from Daniel Keyes' *Flowers for Algernon*). P: Arthur Ornitz. M: Ravi
Shankar.
Clockwork Orange, A. Britain, 1971 (Warner). D, S: Stanley Kubrick (from
Anthony Burgess). P: John Alcott. M: Walter Carlos, and (from) Beetho-
ven, Purcell, Rossini, Elgar, etc.
Creature from the Black Lagoon, The. USA, 1954 (Universal). D: Jack
Arnold. S: Harry Essex, Arthur Ross. P (3D): William E. Snyder, James
E. Havens. M: Joseph Gershenson, Hans J. Salter.
Creeping Unknown, The (The Quatermass Experiment). Britain, 1955
(United Artists). D: Val Guest. S: Richard Landau, Guest (from Nigel
Kneale's TV serial). P: Walter Harvey. M: James Bernard.
Damned, The (These Are the Damned). Britain, 1961 (Columbia). D:
Joseph Losey. S: Evan Jones (from H. L. Lawrence's *Children of Light*).
P: Arthur Grant. M: James Bernard.
Day Mars Invaded Earth, The. USA, 1962 (Fox). D: Maury Dexter. S:
Harry Spaulding. P: John Nikolaus, Jr. M: Richard LaSalle.
Day the Earth Stood Still, The. USA, 1951 (Fox). D: Robert Wise. S: Ed-
mund H. North (from Harry Bates's *Farewell to the Master*). P: Leo
Tover. M: Bernard Herrmann.
Destination Moon. USA, 1950 (United Artists). D: Irving Pichel. S: Rip
Van Ronkel, Robert A. Heinlein, James O'Hanlon (from Heinlein's
Rocketship Galileo). P: Lionel Lindon. M: Leith Stevens. Pr: George
Pal.

[1] D = director. S = scriptwriter. P = photographer. Eff = special effects by.
M = music by. Des = set design by. Pr = producer.

Doctor Cyclops. USA, 1940 (Paramount). D: Ernest B. Schoedsack. S: Tom Kilpatrick. P: Henry Sharp, Winton C. Hoch. Eff: Farciot Edouart, Wallace Kelley. M: Ernest Toch, Gerald Carbonara, Albert Hay Malotte.

Fahrenheit 451. Britain, 1966 (Universal). D: François Truffaut. S: Truffaut, Jean-Louis Richard (from Ray Bradbury). P: Nick Roeg. M: Bernard Herrmann.

Fantastic Voyage. USA, 1966 (Fox). D: Richard Fleischer. S: Harry Kleiner, David Duncan. P: Ernest Laszlo. Eff: L. B. Abbott, Art Cruickshank, Emil Kosa, Jr. M: Leonard Rosenman.

Final War, The. Japan, 1962. D: Hidaka Toshiaki. S: Kyusan Kai.

Fin du Monde, La. France, 1931. D, S: Abel Gance (from Camille Flammarion). P: Jules Kruger, Nicholas Roudakoff.

Five. USA, 1951 (Columbia). D, S: Arch Oboler. P: Louis Clyde Stoumen, Ed Spiegel, Arthur Swerdloff. M: Henry Russell.

Five Million Years to Earth (Quatermass and the Pit). Britain, 1967 (Fox). D: Roy Ward Baker. S: Nigel Kneale (from his TV serial). P: Arthur Grant. M: Tristram Cary.

Forbidden Planet. USA, 1956 (MGM). D: Fred McLeod Wilcox. S: Cyril Hume. P: George Folsey. M: Louis and Bebe Barron. Des: Cedric Gibbons, Arthur Lonergan.

F.P.1. Does Not Answer. Germany, 1932. D: Karl Hartl. S: Walter Reisch, Kurt Siodmak (from Thea von Harbou). P: Gunther Rittau, Konstantin Tschet. M: Allan Gray. Pr: Erich Pommer.

Frau im Mond, Die. Germany, 1929. D: Fritz Lang. S: Thea von Harbou. Adviser: Hermann Oberth. P: Curt Courant, Oskar Fischinger, Otto Kanturek, Konstantin Tschet.

Gladiators, The. Sweden, 1970. D: Peter Watkins. S: Watkins, Nicholas Gosling. P: Peter Suschitzky.

Glen and Randa. USA, 1971 (UMC). D: Jim McBride. S: Lorenzo Mans, Rudolph Wurlitzer, McBride. P: Alan Raymond.

Godzilla. Japan, 1955 (Columbia). D: Inoshiro Honda. S: Takeo Murata, Honda. P: Maseo Tamai. Eff: Eiji Tsuburuya. M: Akira Hukube.

Human Duplicators, The. USA, 1964 (Allied Artists). D: Hugo Grimaldi. S: Arthur C. Pierce. P: Monroe Askins.

Ikarie XB 1 (Voyage to the End of the Universe). Czechoslovakia, 1963 (American International). D: Jindrich Polak. S: Polak, Pavel Juracek. P: Jan Kalis. M: Zdenek Liska. Des: Jan Zazvorka.

Incredible Shrinking Man, The. USA, 1957 (Universal). D: Jack Arnold. S: Richard Matheson (from his book). P: Ellis W. Carter. M: Joseph Gershenson. Eff: Clifford Stine. Des: Alexander Golitzen, Robert Clatworthy.

Invasion of the Body Snatchers. USA, 1956 (Allied Artists). D: Don Siegel. S: Daniel Mainwaring (from Jack Finney's *The Body Snatchers*). P: Ellsworth Fredricks. M: Carmen Dragon.

Invisible Man, The. USA, 1933 (Universal). D: James Whale. S: R. C. Sherriff, Philip Wylie (from H. G. Wells). P: Arthur Edeson. Eff: John P. Fulton.

Island of Lost Souls, The. USA, 1933 (Paramount). D: Erle C. Kenton. S: Waldemar Young, Philip Wylie (from H. G. Wells's *The Island of Dr. Moreau*). P: Karl Struss.

It Came from Outer Space. USA, 1953 (Universal). D: Jack Arnold. S: Harry Essex (from Ray Bradbury). P (3D): Clifford Stine.

Je t'aime, je t'aime. France, 1968 (Fox). D: Alain Resnais. S: Jacques Sternberg. P: Jean Boffety. M: Krzysztof Penderecki.

Jetée, La. France, 1963. D, S: Chris Marker. P: Jean Ravel. M: Trevor Duncan.

Man's Genesis. USA, 1911. D: D. W. Griffith.

Metropolis. Germany, 1926. D: Fritz Lang. S: Thea von Harbou (from her book). P: Karl Freund, Gunther Rittau. Des: Otto Hunte, Erich Kettelhut, Karl Vollbrecht. Pr: Erich Pommer.

Night of the Living Dead, The. USA, 1968 (Reade). D: George A. Romero. S: Romero, John Russo.

1984. Britain, 1956 (Columbia). D: Michael Anderson. S: William P. Templeton, Ralph Bettinson (from George Orwell). P: C. Pennington-Richards. M: Malcolm Arnold.

Omicron. Italy, 1963. D, S: Ugo Gregoretti. P: Carlo di Palma. M: Piero Umiliani.

On the Beach. USA, 1959 (United Artists). D: Stanley Kramer. S: John Paxton (from Nevil Shute). P: Giuseppe Rotunno. M: Ernest Gold.

Paris Qui Dort. France, 1923. D, S: René Clair. P: Maurice Desfassiaux, Paul Guichard.

Planet of the Apes. USA, 1968 (Fox). D: Franklin J. Schaffner. S: Michael Wilson, Rod Serling (from Pierre Boulle). P: Leon Shamroy. M: Jerry Goldsmith.

Robinson Crusoe on Mars. USA, 1964 (Paramount). D: Byron Haskin. S: Ib Melchior, John C. Higgins. P: Winton C. Hoch. M: Van Cleave. Pr: George Pal.

Silent Running. USA, 1972 (Universal). D: Douglas Trumbull. S: Deric Washburn, Mike Cimino, Steve Bochco. P: Charles F. Wheeler. M: Peter Schickele.

Tenth Victim, The. Italy, 1965. D: Elio Petri. S: Petri, Ennio Flaiano, Tonino Guerra, Giorgio Salvione (from Robert Sheckley's "The Seventh Victim"). P: Gianni di Venanzo. M: Piero Piccioni.

Them! USA, 1954 (Warner). D: Gordon Douglas. S: Ted Sherdeman. P: Sid Hickox. M: Bronislau Kaper.

Thing from Another World, The. USA, 1951 (RKO). D: Christian Nyby. S: Charles Lederer (from John W. Campbell, Jr.'s "Who Goes There?"). P: Russell Harlan. M: Dimitri Tiomkin. Pr: Howard Hawks.

Things to Come. Britain, 1936 (United Artists). D: William Cameron Menzies. S: H. G. Wells. P: George Périnal. M: Arthur Bliss. Des: Vincent Korda. Eff: Ned Mann, Harry Zech. Pr: Alexander Korda.

This Island Earth. USA, 1955 (Universal). D: Joseph Newman. S: Franklin Coen, Edward O'Callaghan (from Raymond F. Jones). P: Clifford Stine. M: Herman Stein. Des: Alexander Golitzen, Richard H. Riedel.

THX 1138. USA, 1971 (Warner). D: George Lucas. S: Lucas, Walter Murch. P: Dave Meyers, Albert Kihn. M: Lalo Schifrin. Des: Michael Haller.

Time Machine, The. USA, 1960 (MGM). D: George Pal. S: David Duncan, Philip Yordan (from H. G. Wells). P: Paul C. Vogel. M: Russell Garcia. Eff: Gene Warren, Tim Barr.

Time Travelers, The. USA, 1964 (American International). D, S: Ib Melchior. P: William Zsigmond. M: Richard LaSalle.

Transatlantic Tunnel. Britain, 1934. D: Maurice Elvey. S: Kurt Siodmak, Clemence Dane. P: Gunther Krampf.

Trip to the Moon, A. France, 1902. D. S: Georges Méliès.

20,000 Leagues Under the Sea. USA, 1916. D: Stuart Paton. P: Eugene Gaudio. Eff: J. E. Williamson.

20,000 Leagues Under the Sea. USA, 1955 (Buena Vista). D: Richard Fleischer. S: Earl Felton (from Jules Verne). P: Frank Planer, Till Gabbani. M: Paul Smith.

2001: A Space Odyssey. Britain, 1968 (MGM). D: Stanley Kubrick. S: Kubrick, Arthur C. Clarke (from Clarke's "The Sentinel"). P: Geoffrey Unsworth. M: (from) Richard Strauss, Johann Strauss, Aram Khachaturian, Gyorgy Ligeti. Eff: Kubrick, Wally Veevers, Douglas Trumbull, Con Pederson, Tom Howard.

Unearthly Stranger. Britain, 1962 (American International). D: John Krish. S: Rex Carlton. P: Reg Wyer. M. Edward Williams.

Village of the Damned. Britain, 1960 (MGM). D: Wolf Rilla. S: Rilla, Stirling Silliphant, George Barclay (from John Wyndham's *The Midwich Cuckoos*). P: Geoffrey Faithfull. M: Ron Goodwin.

War Game, The. Britain, 1965. D, S: Peter Watkins. P: Peter Bartlett.

War of the Worlds. USA, 1953 (Paramount). D: Byron Haskin. S: Barré Lyndon (from H. G. Wells). P: George Barnes. M: Leith Stevens. Eff: Gordon Jennings, Wallace Kelley, Paul Lerpae, Ivyl Burts, Jan Donela, Irmin Roberts. Pr: George Pal.

When Worlds Collide. USA, 1951 (Paramount). D: Rudolph Maté. S: Sydney Boehm (from Edwin Balmer, Philip Wylie). P: John F. Seitz. M: Leith Stevens. Des: Hal Pereira, Albert Nozaki. Pr: George Pal.

Wonderful Invention, The (The Fabulous World of Jules Verne). Czechoslovakia, 1958 (Warner). D, Eff: Karel Zeman. S: Zeman, F. Hrubin (from Jules Verne). M: Z. Liska.

World Without End. USA, 1956 (Allied Artists). D, S: Edward Bernds. P: Ellsworth Fredricks. M: Leith Stevens.

X—The Man with X-Ray Eyes. USA, 1963 (American International). D: Roger Corman. S: Robert Dillon, Ray Russell. P: Floyd Crosby. M: Les Baxter.

Bibliography

A., G.L. Notice of *Them!* *Twentieth Century* (September 1954): 197–98.
Condemns the film as an unpleasantly horrific anti-communist allegory.

Agel, Jerome. *The Making of Kubrick's "2001."* New York: Signet Film
Series, 1970. Some interesting material amid a hash of reviews, production information, and various snippets.

Amis, Kingsley. *New Maps of Hell.* New York: Harcourt Brace Jovanovich,
1960. Ambivalent appraisal of SF literature with some incidental mention of films.

*Anonymous. Notice of *Things to Come.* *Journal of the British Interplanetary Society* (February 1937). Assails scientific impossibility of the
space gun.

*Anonymous. "Schoedsack Tells of Making *Dr. Cyclops.*" *American Cinematographer* 21 (April 1940): 158. Tells how the actors were "miniaturized."

Baxter, John. *Science Fiction in the Cinema.* New York: International Film
Guide Series, 1970. Comprehensive historical and critical survey, with
filmography.

*Bessy, Maurice. *Méliès.* Paris: L'Avant-Scene/C.I.B. (Anthologie du
Cinéma series), 1967. A useful overview of Méliès's life, work, and place
in film history.

Bessy, Maurice and Lo Duca. *Georges Méliès, Mage,* rev. ed. Paris: Pauvert,
1961. Copiously illustrated study of Méliès's life and work, with scripts
and other documentary material.

Bouyxou, J. P. *La Science Fiction au Cinéma.* Paris: Union Générale
d'Éditions, 1971. A mixed blessing: some good historical and background
material submerged in opinionated rhetoric.

*Bowen, Elizabeth. *"Things to Come;* A Critical Appreciation." *Sight and
Sound* 17 (Spring 1936): 10–12. Generally favorable review, noting the
film's impression of size and its use of sound.

*Braucourt, Guy. "Entretien avec Donald Siegel." *Image et Son* 238 (April
1970): 80–83. Includes a discussion of *Invasion of the Body Snatchers.*

*Ciment, Michel. "L'Odyssée de Stanley Kubrick; III—Vers I'Infini."
Positif 98 (October 1968): 14–20. Appraises *2001* in relation to Kubrick's
earlier work (which is examined in Parts I and II).

"Cinema e Fantascienza." *Cinema Domani* 4–5 (July–October 1962): 5–19.
A questionnaire on SF films with answers by various filmmakers (in-

* Denotes selection reprinted in this Volume.

cluding Antonioni, Godard, Truffaut, Petri). See also "Fantascienza e Cinema."

Clarens, Carlos. *An Illustrated History of the Horror Film*. New York: Putnam, 1968. Two chapters survey the SF film since World War II; filmography.

Clarke, Arthur C. *The Lost Worlds of 2001*. New York: New American Library, 1972. Excerpts from progressive drafts of the novel on which the script was based, with background comments.

*Clarke, Arthur C. "When Worlds Collide." *Journal of the British Interplanetary Society* (January 1952): 1–3. Regrets a falling off from the authenticity of *Destination Moon*.

Cleaver, A. V. "*Destination Moon*." *Journal of the British Interplanetary Society* (September 1950): 241–4. Praise for the film's technical accuracy. This issue also contains a crushing notice of *Rocketship XM*.

Cooke, Alistair. "*Things to Come*." *The Listener* (March 18, 1936): 545–6. Reprinted in Alistair Cooke, *Garbo and the Night Watchmen* (1937). Thoughtful appraisal of the film's visual strength and prophetic weakness.

"Fantascienza e Cinema." *Cinema Domani* 6 (November–December 1962): 5–18; 7 (January–February 1963): 15–29; 8 (March–April 1963): 19–25. A questionnaire on SF films with answers by various SF writers (including Aldiss, Ballard, Bradbury). See also "Cinema e Fantascienza."

*Gauthier, Guy. "Musée Imaginaire de la Science Fiction." *Image et Son* 194 (May 1966): 40–44. An unusual approach to some of the aesthetic problems and possibilities of the SF film.

*Geduld, Harry M. "Return to Méliès: Reflections on the Science Fiction Film." *The Humanist* (November–December 1968): 23–8. Considers *2001* in the light of historical trends in the SF film.

*Heinlein, Robert A. "Shooting *Destination Moon*." *Astounding Science Fiction* (July 1950): 6–18. Lively description of Heinlein's experiences as technical adviser on the film.

*Hodgens, Richard. "A Brief, Tragical History of the Science Fiction Film." *Film Quarterly* 13 (Winter 1959): 30–39. A sharply critical survey of SF films of the 1950s.

Houston, Penelope. "Glimpses of the Moon." *Sight and Sound* 22 (April–June 1953): 185–8. An appraisal of post-World War II developments in the SF film.

Huss, Roy and T. J. Ross. *Focus on the Horror Film*. Englewood Cliffs, N.J.: Prentice-Hall, 1972. Part of the same series as the present volume; includes a section on monster films.

Knight, Arthur. "Wise in Hollywood." *Saturday Review* (August 8, 1970): 22–5. On the making of *The Andromeda Strain*.

Knight, Damon. *In Search of Wonder*. rev. ed. Chicago: Advent, 1967. Critical studies of SF writing, with disembowelings of some films and books on which films are based.

*Kyrou, Ado. "La Science et la Fiction." *Positif* 24 (May 1957): 29–32. SF seen as a liberating force.

Laclos, Michel. *Le Fantastique au Cinéma*. Paris: Pauvert, 1958. Heavily illustrated; the brief text has some useful observations on the relation of SF to fantasy.

*Laura, Ernesto G. "Invasione degli Ultracorpi." *Bianco e Nero* 18 (December 1957): 69–71. Sees *Invasion of the Body Snatchers* as a basically McCarthyite film.

Lee, Walter W., Jr. *Science Fiction and Fantasy Film Checklist.* Los Angeles: Lee, 1958. Listing with partial credits; annotated for various fantasy genres, with a loose interpretation of SF. Lee is now publishing a greatly expanded version: *Reference Guide to Fantastic Films.*

Ley, Willy. *Rockets, Missiles, & Men in Space,* 4th ed. New York: Viking, 1968. Includes a passage on Oberth's association with *Die Frau im Mond.*

*Lightman, Herb A. "Filming *2001: A Space Odyssey.*" *American Cinematographer* 49 (June 1968): 412–47. A description of various technical aspects of the film, based on an interview with Kubrick. This issue also contains other articles on the making of *2001.*

McConnell, Frank. "Rough Beast Slouching: A Note on Horror Movies." *Kenyon Review* 128, no. 1 (1970): 109–20. Academic and perverse but stimulating survey that covers such films as *Them!* and *Invasion of the Body Snatchers.*

*Mogno, Dario. "Trieste: Il Primo Festival dalla Fantascienza." *Bianco e Nero* 24 (July–August 1963): 96–109. Reflections on the nature of SF, followed by an appraisal of the entries at the First Science Fiction Film Festival.

Pal, George. "Filming *War of the Worlds.*" *Astounding Science Fiction* (October 1953): 100–111. Describes technical effects and gives other background information.

*Ramsaye, Terry. *A Million and One Nights.* New York: Simon & Schuster, 1926. Chapter 12, "Paul and *The Time Machine,*" studies the relationship between Wells and the early cinema.

Ranieri, Tino. "Trieste: Rassegna utile con qualche Incertezza." *Bianco e Nero* 26 (October–November 1965): 87–103. Thorough critical report on the third Trieste festival. Ranieri also reported on later festivals in *Bianco e Nero.*

Rogers, Ivor A. "Extrapolative Cinema." *Arts in Society* VI (summer–fall 1969): 287–291. Finds the most vital examples of SF in films of political, social, and philosophical speculation or satire.

Sadoul, Georges. *Georges Méliès.* Paris: Seghers, 1961. Includes biography, texts by Méliès, and detailed filmography.

Histoire Générale du Cinéma. Paris: Denoël, 1951. Part III, *Le Cinéma Devient un Art,* vol. 1, *L'Avant-Guerre,* includes detailed information on various precursors of SF.

Sawyer, E. V. "The Moon—One Step Nearer." *Pacific Rockets: Journal of the Pacific Rocket Society* (Summer–Fall 1949): 23–6. Describes a visit to the set of *Destination Moon.* The issue contains other articles by members of the PRS who visited the set.

"Science Fiction." *Image et Son* 194 (May 1966): 16–21. A round table discussion with Alain Dorémieux, Jean-Claude Romer, Guy Gauthier, Guy Allombert, François Chevassu, Michel Ciment, Raymond Lefèvre, and Jacques Zimmer on the nature of the SF film.

*Scot, Darrin. "Filming *The Time Machine.*" *American Cinematographer* 41 (August 1960): 490–98. Describes various technical effects, especially those conveying time travel.

Siclier, Jacques, and André S. Labarthe. *Images de la Science Fiction.* Paris: Éditions du Cerf, 1958. Still a useful historical survey, viewing SF films in the light of both the cinema in general and world events.

Sontag, Susan. "The Imagination of Disaster." *Commentary* 40 (October 1965): 42–8. Reprinted in somewhat revised form in Sontag, *Against Interpretation* (1965). A sociological interpretation of post-World War II SF films.

Tarratt, Margaret. "Monsters from the Id." *Films and Filming* (December 1970): 38–42; (January 1971): 40–42. A freewheeling Freudian interpretation of selected SF films of the 1950s.

*Truffaut, François. Review of *Dr. Cyclops. Cahiers du Cinéma* 25 (July 1953): 58. A brief, offbeat appraisal.

* "Journal de *Fahrenheit 451*." *Cahiers du Cinéma* 176 (March 1966): 20–30; 177 (April 1966): 21–24; 178 (May 1966): 17–24; 179 (June 1966): 17–24; 180 (July 1966): 15–18. On-the-set experiences and off-the-set reflections.

Wells, H. G. "Mr. Wells Reviews a Current Film." *The New York Times* (April 17, 1927): IV: 4, 22. Reprinted as "The Silliest Film" in Wells, *The Way the World Is Going* (1928). An onslaught against the socioeconomic weakness of *Metropolis.*

**Things to Come.* London: Cresset Press, 1953. The preproduction screenplay, with introductory comments by Wells.

Whitfield, Stephen E., and Gene Roddenberry. *The Making of "Star Trek."* New York: Ballantine, 1968. Gossipy and repetitive, with much information peculiar to TV; but gives useful insights into the production side of SF films.

Williamson, J. E. *Twenty Years Under the Sea.* London: John Lane, 1935. A breezy autobiography by a pioneer of underwater photography, including an extensive account of the making of the 1916 version of *20,000 Leagues Under the Sea.*

Youngblood, Gene. *Expanded Cinema.* New York: Dutton, 1970. A study of recent trends in experimental cinema, with two chapters on *2001.*

Index[1]

[1] The index does not cover the Chronology, Filmography, or Bibliography.